Dealing with Differences

DEALING
WITH DIFFERENCES

Nico Vink

KIT PUBLISHERS — AMSTERDAM

Dealing with Differences, Nico Vink, PhD
Original Dutch title: *Grenzeloos communiceren*, Nico Vink.
Published in 2001 by KIT Publishers

KIT Publishers
Mauritskade 63
Postbus 95001
1090 HA Amsterdam
E-mail: publishers@kit.nl

Websites:
www.kit.nl/publishers
www.hotei-publishing.com

© 2005 KIT Publishers – Amsterdam

Lay-out: Henny Scholten, Amsterdam.
Cover: Nico Richter, Monnickendam.
Photo cover (front): Peter Adams, Zefa, Amsterdam
Production: Meester and De Jonge, Lochem.
Editor: Shirley Agudo, Pro/PR, Laren.

ISBN 90 6832 588 4
NUR 812/ 741/ 780

Books on Intercultural communication available at
KIT Publishers (in English):
Dealing with the Dutch, J. Vossestein
Living with the Dutch, Norean Radke Sharpe
Unlocking the Secret of Otherland, Mieke Janssen Matthes

Books on Intercultural communication available at
KIT Publishers (in Dutch):
Grenzeloos communiceren, N. Vink
Vreemd volk, J. Vossestein
ExpatHandboek, J. Vossestein, N. Vink *et al.*
Een bestaan als expatriate, F. Quarles van Ufford
Wereldkids, M. Zoer
Het geheim van Anderland, Mieke Janssen Matthes

CONTENTS

Chapter 1

INTRODUCTION

The urgency of an alternative approach in intercultural communication (IC) Jokes about neighbouring nations are popular all over the world, making people's neighbours appear either stupid or canny. According to Christie Davis, an expert on joking, the stupidity jokes are generally pinned on a familiar group, one similar to the joke teller but who lives at the periphery of the teller's country or culture. Examples are the Canadian jokes about Newfoundlanders, the English and Scottish about the Irish, the French about the French Swiss, the Italians about their southern compatriots, the Indians and Pakistani about the Sikhs, South Africans about the Afrikaners, and the Dutch about the Belgians.[1] A typical example of the last category is the following joke:

In a police station, three men stand in a line-up, suspected of
armed robbery of a jeweller: a German, a Dutchman and a
Belgian. The shop owner enters the station in order to identify
the culprit. Then the Belgian steps out of the row and says,
'Yes, it is him.'[2]

Whether you like this joke or not, it reveals to us a stereotype, and is not intended as a guide to dealing with Belgians. Travelling as a tourist in Belgium, you would not want to project the implied image. Belgians can be clever or stupid as well as everything in between. Still, a lot of intercultural manuals are based on generalizations related to stereotypes and suppose that we apply them in intercultural communication. They teach us labels such as: the French have a lot of respect for hierarchies; the Germans are very precise; the Brazilians are corporal and expressive; and so on.

Many travel guides inform travellers about how to avoid communication problems during their holidays abroad. Books on 'culture shock' in various countries help them. Foreigners visiting or working in The Netherlands, for example, are assisted with the bestseller *Dealing with the Dutch*. Managers wanting to cope with an international workforce dispose of similar resources, and books written by scholars like Hofstede offer them guidelines on how to cope with cross-cultural management problems.

The assumption underlying both the popular and more academic books is the same: the existence and crucial role of national cultures. These are defined by mutual comparison of certain value dimensions, synthesized in a basic score of those dimensions, like the opposition of 'individualism-collectivism' or a combination of those dimensions, e.g., uncertainty-avoidance, masculinity and hierarchy. The manager or traveller who has internalised these scores should be able to cope with the cultural differences. Such books are bestsellers and the training sessions well frequented. However, *are* the assumptions correct? Is the concept of national cultures in accordance with the current reality of a global world?

Or is there an alternative approach for intercultural communication that does not focus on national cultures? Another current of theoreticians in intercultural communication, like Gudykunst and Kim, focus their approach on the problems people feel in communicating with strangers. For them, the problems that arise when a person finds him or herself in an unfamiliar environment are typical for intercultural communication. By 'communicating with strangers', they mean communicating with people that are unknown and unfamiliar, including not only people from another nation but also people from their own (sub)-culture who are in an environment new to them.

Let us check if this approach works by looking at another case. You know the tragic/comic story of a French boy on an American Airlines flight who was arrested and put in prison for more than a week because of a remark to the American stewardess. She had become angry when he used the toilet for too long and, while sitting near each other during the landing, the Frenchman said to her: 'My shit doesn't explode.'(!) After the landing he was arrested at Kennedy Airport and interrogated, as she had understood him to say: 'Shit, it doesn't explode.'[3] Is this a typical example of miscommunication between a Frenchmen and a North American? No doubt there was a language problem. But Gudykunst would probably use another explanation not so much based on national differences – something like the problem of a Frenchman in an unfamiliar situation. Could he better explain what went wrong between the boy and the flight attendant? I do not think so. Both partners in this miscommunication are in the same situation: reasonably familiar, certainly not strange. In order to understand this problem, we should take into account the context of the story that is, in this case, really global: the influence of the September 11th terrorist attacks and the fear in the USA of its repetition. Communication, successful or not, has always to be seen in its context. Today this context is often global, too.

This book defends the rather bold thesis that both traditional approaches are outdated. They are no longer sufficient to explain today's problems of intercultural communication or to help people cope with them. The world has changed so much that those approaches, developed in quite different circumstances, cannot explain what is happening in this globalizing world. This book's point of departure is that only when we take globalisation and its consequences seriously can we understand and practice intercultural communication effectively today.

Globalisation The introduction of the concept of globalisation does not immediately help to make things simple. It is a rather complex concept. The discussion about what globalisation could be has not finished; it is easier to say what globalisation is not. The anti-global movement has attacked globalisation as the ideology of the global market. That is not the definition of globalisation used here. In order to avoid misunderstandings, it would help to call this understanding of the term 'globalism', the ideology of globalisation. How to define globalisation? At least among sociologists, a certain consensus has been reached. They speak of a true socio-cultural change affecting all dimensions of social reality. All fields or dimensions are connected and influence each other. It is a multidimensional concept covering technology, social relations, communication,[4] place and time, and, not in the least, economy.

For John Tomlinson, globalisation is 'complex connectivity' because the concept 'refers to the rapidly developing, and ever-densening network of interconnections and interdependencies that characterises modern social life.'[5] In this book we focus on the cultural dimension. What are the consequences of this process on culture? 'Globalisation denotes the stretching and deepening of social relations and institutions across space and time such that, on the one hand, day to day activities are increasingly influenced by events happening on the other side of the globe and, on the other hand, the practice and decisions of local groups can have significant global reverberations.'[6] A war in Afghanistan has an impact on everyone's daily life. Photos taken in an Iraqi prison can cause a political crisis in the USA. This means that we should abandon the idea of separate local, national and global spheres, and replace it by an inclusive understanding which sees each of them as spaces that are linked to and influence each other. It also contains the double movement of de-localisation and re-localisation. It has proven that the thesis of 'Macdonaldisation' of the world is too superficial. The idea of the growth of a global homogeneous culture in which all cultural products are produced and consumed in the same way is not accurate. It is a lot more complicated; we see a global homogenisation of culture simultaneously with the local heterogenisation of cultural traditions. In Brazil, McDonalds introduced the Mc-Carnival and in The Netherlands the Mc-Croquette, adapting to local specificities. Beck illustrates this double process by the hilarious example of the Bavarian *Weiswurst- Hawai*, a combination of traditional regional food in a global new form.[7]

Concentrating on the influence of globalisation on culture and communication, I believe the following elements are crucial:

First, goods are being produced not just in one place but all over the world. Therefore, it is no longer possible to know where an industrial good, such as a car, has been produced. The same can be said of cultural goods. They are also put together by using elements originating from various places and, increasingly, from various continents. The consequence of this process is not only that the importance of 'the national' or 'the authentic' cultures has disappeared, but also that people are becoming consumers who exercise their citizenship not so much politically but in their consumption.[8]

Secondly, as a result of this process, a new middle class has emerged which is involved in the management of knowledge and information; a class characterised by a new ethos and new patterns of consumption. This class does not regard life only as an opportunity to work but rather as a project of self-realisation.[9] Such a personal project depends on the situation, especially on the life partners in the ongoing communication. Flexible adaptation to others creates a life in plural. Individual identity is no longer simple and stable but in permanent flux and multiple. As with their body and lifestyle, people can and should also change and permanently adapt their presentation of self.

Thirdly, as we look at culture as the industrial production of cultural goods, we see that the electronic media, TV and network have become predominant. The traditional opposition between elite and popular culture has almost disappeared. In modern time, they were each other's opposites, yet now they mix. Both artists and consumers mix a variety of products and styles. Examples of this trend, e.g. in Latin-America, are Piazzola's tangos, Tom Jobin's 'Bossa nova' and the romances of Puig. The separation between high and popular culture tends to disappear. Orestes' last tango is not only a combination of classical Greek drama, opera and tango but also a product of co-operation between Dutch and Argentine artists. Professionals in the field of visual arts, like Andy Warhol, borrow from here, there and everywhere, including industrial mass production. This development has brought about a redefinition of the popular and the elite culture. In the urban centres, hybridisation or exchange of cultures is taking place – not only horizontally between different regional cultures but also vertically between high and popular culture, especially on TV.

Fourthly, exchange between cultural regions has become more important, i.e. export from the Western world to the 'periphery' and also the inverse. The Indian film industry is today producing more films each year than Hollywood. Cultural exchange has become the rule, so we cannot speak about foreign cultures anymore, nor about 'authentic' cultures, declares Welsh.[10] Cultural themes and elements are taken from their original context and put into new perspectives – not only between (national) cultures, but inside cultures, too.

Fifthly, as said before, globalisation includes de-localisation; cultural traditions lose their traditional context – Islam being a dramatic example of this de-localisation. Islam in London or Amsterdam is experienced differently than in Marrakech or Islamabad. De-localisation takes several forms. Besides the mentioned ways, the presentation of a place becomes, according to Thrift[11], more important than the place itself. It looks as if the meaning of the place has become imprisoned in the media presentation, so that the place itself matters less and less. Rio de Janeiro becomes the statue of Christ the Redeemer or carnival. It has been shown a thousand times. It is 'known', and to be there does not matter that much. Another aspect of de-localisation is what Auge[12] has called the multiplication of *non-places*, i.e., spaces without a history. The increased mobility of millions of people for business or tourism has created many places that look alike everywhere in the world – places without a past and without a link with people. His examples are airport departure lounges, supermarkets, high-speed trains, motorways and service stations. They are places of solitude and anonymity – the contrary of places with an identity. Another example is the big shopping malls – comfortable places to stay, but they lack the human touch and interest of the shops 'next door' where we know the shopkeeper personally.

Sixthly, in the last few years sociologists have demanded attention for another global phenomenon: *trans-national communities*.[13] The increasing numbers of migrants in the world refuse to isolate themselves in the Diaspora; they want to participate in the life of the community of arrival. At the same time, they do not break the links with their country of origin; such migrants remain interested in their mother countries, supporting not only their own families but also the public affairs back home through investment or development projects. The modern means of communication and cheap flights make it easy to remain in touch with their country of origin. These migrants do not live in between two cultures; they participate in at least two at the same time. Reviews of recent articles on trans-nationalism[14] express a wide variety of descriptions and definitions. It has been described as networks, trans-national communities, even (transformed) Diaspora. There is even a specific type of consciousness: 'The majority of the migrants seem to maintain several identities that link them to more than one nation.' The practices typical for these communities are described in terms of syncretism, creolisation and hybridity. They are not only caused by the big players like the trans-national corporations and a trans-national capitalist class. Little players who comprise the bulk of the trans-national communities are making an even greater impact. India and Egypt receive billions, for example, from their compatriots abroad.

So again we would like to emphasise that the dominant process is not globalisation, but glocalisation – a two-way process. The Dutch sociologist Abram de Swaan has summarised this process very well.[15] He perceives global homogenisation next to local heterogenisation. The number of places where cultural products are industrially produced is growing, but at the same time the offer of products in different places becomes more and more similar. Food is a typical example. Almost everywhere you can buy Lebanese falafel, Indian curries and Mexican tacos. But at the same time, all these regional products are integrated into the fast-food sector. Cultural differences increase at the same time as the similarity of cultural products.

Consequences for IC Consequences of globalisation for intercultural communication are obvious; on the one hand, it contradicts the thesis of a national culture. On the other hand, the notions of what is strange and different have to be revised. The traditional 'stranger' has disappeared. The process of globalisation makes the idea of national cultures simplistic and obsolete – useful only for TV serials like Star Trek, where each inter-planetary nation has its own culture and can be identified easily by specific visible biological differences. The Klingons and the Borg can easily be identified. Reality is quite different.

The cultures of Western European nations are not homogeneous, and never have been. Their homogeneous character is a myth, carefully constructed by political elites. Those nations have been multicultural, living together in different ethnic and/or language groups. Only after the invention of the nation state did they become very concerned about building a common culture and language. And, going back to the ethnic joke, it is interesting to realise that before the formation of nation states, those jokes focused on neighbouring villages. Nations are still 'imagined communities' (Anderson). Minorities and other subcultures clash with dominant cultures.

The idea of a Nation-State itself has been questioned. In the last decade of the 20th century, globalisation as a key concept in social sciences indicated a general shift in the perception of the relationship between subject and group. Does globalisation imply the end of the Nation-State? This is still to be discussed, but surely the Nation is losing its central and dominant place at least in social sciences. Ulrich Beck[16] has called the use of the Nation-State as self-evident social space, a 'container theory of society'. The social space is divided arbitrarily into national spaces: French, German or Dutch society, etc. He urges us to look for alternatives. He proposes two other social spaces: trans-national space and world society. Besides that, he advises us not to look for clear-cut distinctions, but to look for mobile and fluid categories.

Trans-national and trans-cultural spaces are concepts that are increasingly used to describe and explain the situation of immigrants. Because, says Portes (1998), migrants are not living in between two cultures – the culture of origin and that of arrival – but participating in two in a specific way at the same time. This brings us to the other tradition in intercultural communication: how to deal with strangers. I have to recognise that this approach always has been sensitive to cultural differences in national cultures and did not limit intercultural communication to national cultures.

However, those ideas about adaptation are developed from the writings of Simmel, a German sociologist living in the early 20th century. My criticism can be summarised in the following points:

1. We don not belong to just one in-group or out-group, but to several of these groups at the same time because, and we will come back later to this point, our identities are plural. Depending on the situation, we can identify with consumers, the voters of a political party, believers, hooligans, pop fans, etc. Our nationality is just one aspect of identity.

2. Another point is that identities change; they are not fixed. This implies another perception of differences. An interview with a Belgian second-generation Moroccan can illustrate this. Majane goes for holidays to her family in Morocco, but she feels like a stranger; she is even called so by her own relatives. She says her daily prayers and wears a scarf, but she is perceived as Belgian and feels not accepted. At the same time she does not understand her nieces wearing swimming suits on the beach and flirting with boys. She perceives them as traitors of Muslim faith and identity. In turn, Majane is conscious of being perceived in Belgium also as a stranger. 'I feel everywhere a stranger. Here I am perceived as a stranger, and in Morocco they call me *bent al khari-j* (daughter from abroad).'[17] In the globalising world, differences between people become fluid, and familiarity with places and people are tested all the time.

3. Finally, strangers are perceived not only negatively, but can be seen as interesting and exciting. The perception by the locals depends on whether they feel threatened in their position or not. People in subordinate positions tend to feel threatened quicker by outsiders than the local elite who have enough resources to defend their position, e.g., 'We will loose our jobs'. The probability of xenophobia is stronger among low-status groups than among others.[18]

I propose in this book to elaborate a new approach for intercultural communication, departing from a combination of Bourdieu's concepts.[19] Three concepts are crucial: the world of common sense, field, and habitus – all three directly related to practices and the production of symbolic goods. Central for Bourdieu is the link between social position in social space and disposition, i.e. perception, appreciation and action – in short, cultural behaviour. Higher and lower positions in social space result in specific frames of mind: visions of reality and self, appreciation of life, and body posture.

Position and disposition   To explain the alternative approach to IC proposed in this book, I like to imagine society as a three-dimensional hierarchical space where everyone occupies a certain position in relation to others: higher or lower, with status or without, far or near, and with little or much social and cultural capital.[20] In real life of democratic societies, socially distant people can meet each other and interact. Nobility nowadays does not marry noble blood. However, this interaction often hides the different positions that the people who interact occupy. The Prince of Orange is perceived by the Dutch public as easy-going because he is 'so simple for a prince' (sic!). The Prince is able to negate the social distance in a way that the distance is recognised by the subjects. Princess Diana has, on the contrary, always remained an outsider, good enough for the continuation of the Windsor bloodline but not really 'one of us'. What determines the relations between people is not so much their interaction but their different positions in social space. These positions are determined by access to economic social and cultural resources. Their positions in the social space, and the groups they belong to, influence the possibility of communicating with others. Their position in relation to each other determines also whether they speak the same language and have the same way of thinking or not. The actors are distributed in the social space firstly according to the volume of each capital, and secondly by the composition of the total capital: more economic and less cultural (captains of industry) or the other way around (university professors). This explains the different positions of the economic and the cultural elites.

The cultural and the economic elites in The Netherlands do not only have quite different lifestyles; they also differ in the places where they choose to live, in the cars they drive, and especially in power and influence.[21] The cultural elite prefer to live in traditional neighbourhoods of Amsterdam; the captains of industry prefer the country-life. Another example of the translation of social distance in the physical space gives us an ethnography of the Tunisian bath. When Tunisian women are taking their bath, apparently they are all equal, but close observation reveals that the poorer women occupy worse positions in this space – where the flowing water is less clean! It is not by accident that immigrants with reduced status are approached as a social problem, and the better-paid professionals are overlooked – so far the objective dimension.

The subjective dimension of sociological analysis recognises that the social position of people shapes their perception of reality; in three words: position shapes disposition. Their social position translates itself into visions of the reality and of themselves.[22] A person's disposition is an embodiment of social conditions – a system of lasting transposable conditions which, integrating past experiences, constantly functions as a matrix of perception, appreciation and action. It can be viewed as the result of the internalisation of the objective conditions an agent or group of agents lives in. Formulated more plastically, it's the whole sum of a person's or group's past experiences: 'Yesterday's man in us.'[23] The original disposition or habitus is shaped within the family in early childhood and, as such, it is the base of later investments in cultural capital and activities. While moving through social space, we reproduce the social conditions of disposition's production. This occurs not automatically but sometimes in unexpected ways. The formation of the disposition is rather complex and will be later discussed in more detail. The most important aspect to remember now in relation to IC is the relationship between position and disposition. How a person thinks and evaluates the world depends on her/his position in the social world. Social differences imply cultural differences.

It is important to emphasise that disposition or attitude is not only about perception and knowledge. Social identities of people and groups are also involved. The differences in social positions produce not only different dispositions and visions but also the various categories used to order social life. Categories like 'women', 'poor', 'black', and 'young' are used to give sense to the world, to name the differences and similarities between people and label them. Those labels are not facts, but they are used to construct social reality like social class, family or nation. Categories or labels are used in the continuous struggle to shape and change the vision of reality. Social classes don't exist as such, but using the label of 'working class' is a way to mobilise such groups. In the 80s, the contra-revolutionaries active in Nicaragua were baptised by President Reagan as 'Freedom Fighters'. Concepts like 'nation', 'region', 'class' and 'family' are also weapons in the struggle between groups in politics and social sciences to impose their view on reality. Categories are not facts but stakes of struggle; they are used to construct reality, to organise groups and to change their positions in the social field. Look at the use of the word 'nigger' in the recent history of the USA. Once identified as pure white racism, for the rap-musician it has become a sign of identity.[24] Or more dramatically, look at the recent history of national identities in the Balkan.

On the other hand, we do not perceive certain parts of reality because we do not have names for them. Remember the absurd situation when women did not play a role in the development discourse. Female farmers were not mentioned; they disappeared from the map as a specific group and their specific needs were neglected. The consequence was the failure of many agricultural programs. Mental schemas are products of society, but they also produce society.

Because disposition is a translation of one's higher or lower social position in social space, the related visions and tastes are not only different, but they have a different status and influence. Tastemakers and trendsetters tend to be found in the higher positions in society. People low in the social hierarchy accept their position as natural and self-evident. This natural way in which people accept their place in society as self-evident is for Bourdieu 'symbolic power' – not so much the result of conscious manipulation by the elite but of interiorisation of one's subordinate position, often expressed in common sense sayings like, 'That is not for our kind of people.'

Differences between groups can be evaluated positively or negatively. Social existence means to be perceived and to be recognised; exclusion means to be overlooked and to be frozen out. This means that social differences know two basic forms: a positive form and a negative one. With positive forms, the differences are seen and experienced as distinction; the group is morally better and has more rights than others. Development workers, like other expatriates, are seen at least as richer but often also as superior to local population. With negative forms, differences in colour, origin and language are used to stigmatise the bearers of those signs. Some marks are used to put a group in a subordinate position. This happens with migrants, women, homosexuals and others.

Differences still have another dimension. They exist in the eye of others and in the eye of the beholders. They are grounded in reality and at the same time part of the self-image of a group or a person. Together they form the identity of people. How do others perceive them and how do they conceive of themselves? Perception and self-perception are directly related to the social position of people. Some of them have the power to place others, to put them in their place; others can only adapt to their place. How this functions in practice has been nicely described in David Parker's study on the Chinese take-away. Especially the second generation Chinese educated in Britain are capable of analysing their position critically. So explains one of the interviewees, Tsee Sun: 'As a takeaway you are somehow not really 'in' the society . . . I actually felt I am trapped in this little hole full of uncivilized individuals and racist and ignorant people – white English people . . . They don't respect people as an individual, they just see Chinese people as a bunch of cooks who work in our country and provide a service for us as a servant as it were.'[25]

Social identity is part of a struggle between groups in which stigmatised individuals and groups can defend them-selves only by putting emphasis on their best characteristics in their self-definition, or give the dominant categorisation a posi-tive interpretation. What is here at stake is not the truth, but accusation and self-defence, like in a court.[26]

Categorising and stereotyping   According to psycholo-gists, the use of categories is a very human and effective way to process information. Processing so many impressions that a human receives at any moment from all senses is only possible if simplified. Stereotyping would be a logical consequence, as are prejudices, a specific form of stereotyping.[27] Stereotypes have been defined as oversimplified ideas and beliefs about a group of people, in which all individuals of the group are regarded as having the same set of leading characteristics, e.g. homosexuals are sissies, etc. They are considered to be neutral, while preju-dices express an antipathy based on a faulty and inflexible gen-eralisation. Both should, according to Zygmund Bauman, be a consequence and a reinforcement for the existence of in-groups and out-groups distinction – 'them' versus 'us'. Double stan-dards should stimulate emphasis of the homogeneity of the in-group, embellishing their own characteristics and perceiving the 'others' in a negative light.

Are those natural processes that we should accept as normal and self-evident? It seems that human beings can process information in basically two ways: first, a reflexive one in which the information is checked detail for detail and, second, a quick automatic way in which we apply the categories we have learned unconsciously in an uncritical way. Stereotypes are, like prejudices, social constructions. However, stereotypes are not inventions by individuals. 'Individuals construct meaning through discourse and discourse constructs the individual,' according to the psychologist Hinton.[28] Meeting strangers for the first time, we often use an automatic pilot to process information concerning the unknown person; we use the social categories present in our social environment without giving space to individual characteristics of the person. This man is a politician, thus an eloquent flatterer; she is a physician, thus an altruist concerned with mankind. Such stereotypes are human but can hinder real communication. Sociologists like Hall and Foucault explain that stereotyping tends to occur where gross inequalities in power exist. It classifies people according to a norm and constructs the excluded as 'others'. Ruling groups impose their norms of what is normal and accepted through stereotyping. It is a key element in the exercise of symbolic violence.[29]

Stereotyping occurs in the interaction between individuals, but it is more frequent and more outspoken in the public sphere, especially in the media and other forms of representation. Media work with simplifications and selective perception of reality often based on PR information from authorities and enterprises, but presented as objective facts (result of own research by the journalists).[30]

We may conclude that categorising, like stereotyping, is linked with power — unequal positions in society. What are their links with cultures?

Culture as struggle for meaning making   The discussion around intercultural communication is seriously handicapped by the misunderstanding of what culture is. The now common-sense understanding of the word culture goes back to the end of the 18th century. At that time, the German philosopher Herder developed the idea of cultures in the plural. Each folk is characterised by its own national spirit that is inalienable. For Herder the differences between nations are bigger then the similarities between them – ideas that were useful in the construction of the European nation states, accelerating at that time. The development of the nation states and the ideas on national cultures fortified each other.

Today's anthropologists have abandoned this identification of culture and nationality. Culture is for them not any longer the uniform perception of reality by a group but the struggle for perceiving and expressing the social world[31], i.e. culture as a contested process of meaning making. It tells us how concepts are used and contested by actors who occupy different positions in the social space, with unequal power. An example is the acceptance of gay marriage in the USA. Who has the power to define the United State's attitude to homosexuality? Who decides that marriage remains open for heterosexuals only? Or the ardent polemics in The Netherlands and France about who are Muslim and what are their rights? A plurality of viewpoints is daily expressed and struggles for hegemony.

The contemporary anthropological concept of culture is characterised by four elements. Culture is 1. an active process of meaning making; 2. people in different positions use the available resources to impose their definitions of social reality; 3. cultures are never closed systems, they change all the time; 4. besides actors willing to maintain the existing definitions and order, others want to create new names and definitions and so change reality; only in its hegemonic form does a culture appear coherent.[32]

Culture is not something people have as part of their personality, like other things such as eye colour or the curly hair received by genes. It is a whole of traditions and customs that can be changed. In the scientific view, culture is changing all the time as result of struggles between groups trying to impose their view and appreciation of the world. In this process of cultural change, the achievement of new frames of perception and evaluation, formally three different stages, can be distinguished; in stage one, specific agents, politicians, media-workers, and trendsetters redefine key symbols in public discussions, under pressure from interest groups. In the next stage, this change becomes institutionalised, among others by legislation. Finally, the redefined key term becomes part of everyday life and every day's discourse. To use an illustration of such a process: feminists were able to put women's interest on the public agenda; it became a topic in the media. Politicians adapted the legislation in favour of women. Slowly men and women's rights are considered to be equal in common sense. We may conclude that communication is crucial in this process, but at two separated levels: first, in public space by specialists in specific arenas like politics, sciences and media and, secondly, in the world of common sense when elements of the public discussion have naturalised as obvious.

I will try to summarise what we have seen until now by defining culture in Bourdieu's spirit.[33] Culture is the way a (potential) group of people who occupy a similar position in a social space with specific access to economic and cultural goods and services embody this position in their perception, appreciation and behaviour, expressing these in a common lifestyle.

This conceptualisation of culture leaves an important question unanswered. When we talk about (similar) positions, to what space or network of relationships do we refer? Traditionally, anthropologists have used the idea of communities when they did field work in small isolated villages. It was easy then to establish borders. In an urban and globalised world, it is very difficult to establish them. Certainly, national frontiers do not coincide with cultural borders. Globalisation obliges us to challenge the implicit assumptions of a coincidence of cultures, identities and communities. Moreover, social scientists have become inclined to see global cultural variations as continuous. Culture is seen as in flux, contradictory and incoherent, differentially distributed over variously positioned persons, says Ulf Hannerz.[34] Earlier I quoted Beck as defending the adoption of more flexible and fluid categories and proposing concretely trans-national space and world society. Bourdieu uses two different images of social space. He distinguishes between the social space of society and the smaller space of fields, which corresponds to two ways of producing culture: space for everybody and space for the specialists. In the following chapters we analyse this difference, starting with the broader concept of social space. Taking globalisation seriously implies that the nation cannot be the only or even preferred space when we talk about culture. Parallel to global integration and the increasing importance of trans-national levels, we can find an increased interest in local cultural traditions. As we have seen before, globalisation is actually glocalisation. Culture is not only linked to nations, but to a continuum of groups and corresponding spaces. This book will put emphasis on relationships between various and different social spaces, (locality, family/clan, neighbourhood, region, groups, professions, organisations, institutions, nations, continents, and world) and various (sub)-cultures (as behaviour). Those specific social spaces are the context of interaction and determine the possibilities of mutual understanding. Considering the limitations of this book, I will focus on three cultural spaces: local everyday life, global cosmopolitism, and in between both trans-cultural fields.

Intercultural competence As the name of this book indicates, its aim is to help readers to develop their intercultural competence. Later we will discuss how, but it is useful here already to define what is meant by competence. For trainers and educators, it is almost second nature to define the educational goals of their courses and training. What will the students be able to know and to do better once the training has been finished? Training can focus on abilities, knowledge and/ or motivation. This book has didactic objectives, too, and Chapter 6 will explain what and how. But, in advance, here is a brief overview of my intentions. This book does not offer much information about do's and don'ts in communicating with other cultures. The only knowledge I consider essential for IC is self-knowledge; insight into your personal ways of communicating – your strong and weak points and understanding of human communication processes as such. In relation to motivation, I hope to convince the reader, if necessary, that intercultural communication demands openness for those persons who differ from you. Only when we show more interest and respect for others is effective communication, which implies mutual understanding, possible. However, the main focus of this book is on communicative skills. The central message is that the ability to scan positions and relations is crucial to understanding the social position of the other and the distance between them and us, depending on the context, as will be explained in the next chapter. In addition, it helps a lot if we are able to tolerate ambiguity

and to control our first immediate emotions in meeting different people, thereby avoiding common-sense stereotypes.

Content of this book   The structure of this book is a consequence of the mentioned objectives. In this introductory chapter we have explained the central question and purpose of this
book. The second chapter analyses communication as an inter-
active process that demands a continuous scanning of the social
positions and the relations between the parties involved. It is
necessary to reconcile attention to the social background of the
others and their unique character. Nobody is the same; everyone is different. Years ago I met an ex-trainee back again in The
Netherlands after a stay of some years in the Middle East. He
told me that what we had taught during our training was wrong.
He had bluntly checked it with the Arabs themselves. Of course,
my training had failed, right? What matters in communication is
not the information (often based on stereotypes) but interest in
and respect for the other.

In the two subsequent chapters, the social context of communication will be explained in line with the idea of glocalisation. First, Chapter 3 will show the importance of locality for
each person's perception and evaluation of reality, analysing the
concept of everyday culture. I will present it as a flexible concept without fixed boundaries, which should be thought of as
more as a pole of society where the reproduction of the human
existence is at stake – a fluid and a more or less autonomous
space, structured around the pole of the routine activities
aimed at self-reproduction of the person itself, the household
one being part of it. Everyday culture is a consequence of the
primary socialisation in the household/family and an embodiment of its social position not only in society, the Nation-State,
but also in the world. I am convinced that the existence of a
daily-life culture or culture of common sense can explain how
we are socialised and receive our basic disposition which, as
interiorisation of social position of our family or household, will
be the basis of our later value and norm system. The son of a
working class family can become a Cambridge professor but
shall always be influenced by this origin, even denying it. The
daughter of a grocery shopkeeper can, like Margaret Thatcher,
become Prime Minister, but that will be visible in her perfor-

mance and discourse. Although she is now Lady Thatcher, 'It takes three generations to become a gentlemen (and lady).' Our first socialisation influences our culture profoundly and it is difficult to change. We will examine also to what extent globalisation affects everyday-life culture.

Other contexts of communication are cultural fields, the subject of Chapter 4. Fields are micro-universes of cultural production with each a specific commitment with its own theme and rules that demand specific disposition, like artistry or religiosity. Cultural fields are structures mainly in function of the interests of the cultural producers, but they are also implicated in consumption. Their markets, especially of the fields in which cultural goods are produced industrially, can be distinguished between the small avant-garde market of producers and a large market for a large public. The autonomy of field is relative. The boundaries depend on the commitment of the participants on the one hand and the recognition in the field of power on the other. Communication between members of the field is relatively easy because they speak the same language and are driven by the same commitment and disposition. Especially today, since cultural fields like music, fashion, film, etc., are becoming increasingly trans-national, understanding even between strangers is easier.

Globalisation brings about worldwide consumption, but capitalist economy and its related pattern of values, like the spirit of calculation, is not dominant everywhere. The limits of globalisation can be felt when entering in contact with people who are only recently or partly integrated in the world economy. The specific communication problems rising in this situation are the topic of Chapter 5. It focuses on the communication with the poor of the world and religious people.

Chapter 6 will explain how to practically increase one's intercultural competence. In this chapter readers can find methods to increase their own intercultural skills, next to deeper self-knowledge and change of mentality.

The book concludes with a short overview of the way in which Dutch society is dealing with differences, thereby answering the question about the existence of a Dutch national culture. Finally, we will see whether cosmopolitan mentality is a realistic ideal, and under what conditions.

This book will avoid complicating things unnecessarily and will avoid jargon as much as possible but, at the same time, will challenge the reader. Today, intercultural communication is only possible if we break with common sense and mobilise our own creativity to find new ways of mutual understanding.

Notes

1. Christie Davies (1998) *Jokes and their relation to society*. Berlin / New York Mouton de Gruyter.

2. G. Kuipers (2001) *Goede humor, slechte smaak*. Amsterdam, Boom.

3. *Liberation* 26-2-2004 p.40

4. John Tomlinson (1999) *Globalization and culture*. Cambridge, Polity Press; and Ulrich Beck (1999) *Schone Arbeitswelt*; Vision: Weltburgergesellschaft. Frankfurt/ New York, Campus Verlag.

5. Tomlinson o.c. p.2. *Democracy and Global order*. London, Polity Press.

6. David Held (1995: p.20), building on Giddens' concept of time – space shrinkage.

7. Ulrich Beck o.c.: p.87.

8. Nestor Garcia Canclini (1995) *Consumidores y Cidudadanos*: conflictos multiculturalos de la globalizacion. Mexico, Grijalbo.

9. Pierre Bourdieu (1979) *La Distinction*. Paris du Minuit; M. Featherstone (1999) *Consumer culture and postmodernism*. London etc. Sage.

10. Wofgang Welsh (1999) Transculturality, the puzzling form of cultures today. In: M.Featherstone and S.Lash (eds.) *Spaces of culture*. London, Sage.

11. Thrift, Nigel (1997) 'Us and Them'; reimagening places, reimagening identities.
In: H. Mackay *Consumption and everyday life*. London Sage: pp.159- 212.

12. Marc Auge (1995) *Non-places;* introduction to an anthropology of supermodernity. London, Verso.

13. See Alejandro Portes (1999) La mondialisation par le bas. In: *Actes de la Recherches en Sciences Sociales* n.129 sept.

14. Steven Vertovec (2001) transnational challenges to the 'New' Multiculturalism. *Working papers E.S.R.C.* See: www.transcomm.ox.ac.uk.

15. Abram de Swaan (1995) De sociologische studie van de transnationale samenleving. In: Heilbron en Wilterdink (eds.) *Mondialisering*. Groningen Wolters-Noordhoff.

16. Ulrich Beck (2000) the sociological perspective: sociology of the second age of modernity. In: *British Journal of Sociology* 50/1: pp.79-105.

17. Nadia Fadil (2003) Dochters van het buitenland. In: M.C. Foblets e.a. (eds) *Migratie zijn wij uw kinderen?* p.30.

18. Manfred Bornewasser (1993) Social psychological reactions to social change and instability. In: *Civilisations* 42/2: pp. 91 – 103.

19. Although all of his books finally speak about culture, Bourdieu has never shown interest in conceptualising culture as such. This book will attempt to develop Bourdieu's position in a direction that he has not persisted.

20. Pierre Bourdieu (1994) *Raisons pratiques*. Paris, du Seuil: pp.53 - 57

21. Elleke de Wijs Mulkens (1999) *Wonen op stand*. Amsterdam, Spinhuis.

22. To explain how this is possible, Bourdieu has introduced the concept of 'habitus'. This seems at a first glance somehow strange and even a pedantic concept. Habitus, a recovery of a traditional scholastic expression, is an effort to reconcile the freedom of the individual and the determination exercised by the structures.

23. Bourdieu (1972) *Esquisse d'une theorie de la pratique*. Geneve, Droz: p.178.

24. Kennedy 2001.

25. David Parker (2000) The Chinese Takeaway and the diasporic habitus. In: B. Hesse ed. (2000) *Un/settled multiculturalism*. London/New York, Zed books. p.91

26. Bourdieu (1979) o.c. pp. 554-555.

27. See Wiliam Gudykunst o.c.

28. Perry Hinton o.c. p.143.

29. See Michel Foucault (1975), *Discipline and Punish*. John Fiske (1993) *Power plays, power works*. London, Verso.

30. Cees Hamelink (2004) *Regeert de leugen?* Amsterdam, Boom.

31. See among others Pierre Bourdieu, Anthony Giddens, Stuart Hall, Michel Foucault.

32. See Susan Wright (1998) Politicisation of culture in: *Anthropology in action* V5 1/2.

33. Bourdieu does not use the concept of 'culture'. The impact of habitus takes over, to a large extent, the function of the concept of culture, at least in its subjective aspect. We find the objective material dimension of culture in the symbolic fields where cultural goods are produced, distributed and consumed.

34. Ulf Hannerz (1992) *Cultural complexity*. New York, Columbia University Press.

DEALING WITH DIFFERENCES

Chapter 2

COMMUNICATION AS SCANNING OF SOCIAL SPACES AND POSITIONS

We breathe our whole life. Does this help us to understand the function of our lungs? We are always communicating too, but does that help us to understand how communication works? Just because it is an everyday activity, most people consider themselves communication experts, forgetting that we seldom look critically at our routine activities. We will never understand the specific problems of intercultural communication if we do not understand what personal communication is as such. Although the role of email and TV is increasing, a meeting between two persons is still the primary means of communicating. In recent research conducted in The Netherlands, three quarters of the interviewees said they preferred face-to-face communication when personal matters were involved.[1] Face-to-face communication is a form which can help us to understand how communication works, analysing critically our daily experience. In this chapter I analyse what happens during everyday communication in which, as you will see, cultural differences play a role at all times.

Communication has been studied by a lot of sciences and from quite different perspectives: semiology, sociology, language studies, psychology, and discourse and conversation analysis. The last discipline focuses mainly on the structure of the communication process – such as the fact that each question demands an answer. One of the founders of conversation analysis, Harry Sacks, illustrates the importance of sequences in a conversation with the following Yiddish joke:

A young man is sitting in a train next to a middle-aged man. When the first asks the second if he knows what time it is, the older man answers 'no'. The young fellow, seeing that the other has a watch, asks for an explanation. The older fellow then explains: 'If I tell you what time it is, we start a conversation. You will ask me my destination. It will result that we both are going the same direction. I have to invite you to have a meal at my place. I have at home a young unmarried daughter and I do not want her to marry a boy who cannot afford to buy a watch.' ?

Sacks makes a point in relation to sequences, but he shows something else: the social distance between the partners in this interaction. The father wants to maintain the social distance existing between the young man and his family. This distance is the heart of the conversation and of the joke. It also shows how in a conversation the social context and the text are linked; how the social position of the speakers and the content of the conversation are inseparable. We can analyse and understand a conversation only if we take its context into consideration. Perhaps this is easier to understand if we remember conversations with experts and authorities, e.g., medical doctors or judges. Then we can become aware how differences in position play a crucial role in interactions. This is certainly the case in public life, when authorities speak as official representatives of a group or organisations. But it can also occur in conversations between friends and family when, e.g., one party is male or older, the other party female or younger.

Because the micro and macro dimensions – the psychological and sociological dimensions of communication processes – cannot be separated, we can compare communication competence with the scanning of a radio …testing point for point in order to find the right wavelength in order to get the tune correctly; or, in a medical sense, passing the superficies of the body in order to make the underlying levels visible. In the same way, we should penetrate the superficial layers of conversation, like language and words, in order to understand the relations that are determined at a deeper and more structural level. We think of the social positions of and distance between people, at power relations and identities, and at self- and social perceptions.

Determining one's place in society   Communication studies have popularised the communication model of 'sender- message- receiver'. Even complemented with two other elements, 'feedback' and 'channel', this model remains rather limited. One of the main objections is the unilateral emphasis on transmission of information, i.e. news. The other critique is about its individualistic bias.

Often, everyday conversation does not transmit any news. Researchers like Garfinkel have demonstrated by simple experiments that most of our everyday conversation implies rituals aiming at a confirmation of our good relations. Two colleagues meet each other at the start of a new working day, and this is their exchange: 'Good morning, how are you?' 'Fine, thank you and you?' In French, even shorter: 'Ça va?' 'Ça va!'. The colleague who has been addressed tends to answer always in a positive way, even if things are going wrong, e.g. you did not sleep because your baby was crying the whole night. Starting a new day of work, the colleague is not really interested in listening to your little problems. Interaction here is ritual, not concerned with content. A first meeting with strangers demonstrates more clearly that what really is at stake is relations. What matters in a meeting is to check each other's social position and the social distance between both parties. Where are the parties placed in the social hierarchy, lower or higher or at the same level? Both partners in the conversation check at the same time what the social distance is between them. At the start of such a conversation, a proposition is unconsciously made and later negotiated about how both persons want to see their relation. Who is taking the initiative and who is following? What degree of intimacy are they comfortable with? And this mechanism is not only present in conversations between strangers. A German expert illustrates this by presenting a short dialogue between a couple sitting in a car.[2] She is driving; he is sitting next to his wife/partner. While waiting for the traffic light, he says: 'It's green.' She reacts: 'Who's driving? You or me?' Why this aggressive reaction by the woman? The light was indeed green! This isn't a point of discussion. The woman isn't reacting at the level of the content of the message, but at the level of relation. Right or wrong, her partner has irritated her. Was he pushing her, or perhaps was he sarcastic? Or does she react from a sentiment of inferiority? Whatever the case, her reaction is clear: don't behave like a 'macho', so dominating! She perceives a kind of undesired relationship and reacts accordingly.

Inequality and differences in power can, in private during conversation between lovers or friends, easily be overlooked. That is more difficult in official situations. It is known that Queen Beatrix of The Netherlands is rather conscious of her position, which makes the following story sound plausible. To a departing visitor who said: 'Till the next time,' Beatrix would have answered, 'That depends.' (meaning: on me!), putting this guest in his place.[3] It is her decision as to whom she wants to see. In royal circles this is certainly not new. The French historian Ladurie LeRoy described the everyday life at the court of the French kings. His book shows how the ability to cope with good manners was crucial for maintaining one's position at the Court. Who was allowed to sit down in the presence of the king? And where? On a chair with or without arms, or only on a stool? At a certain moment the game has become so sophisticated that the right on half a stool is at stake.

Those subtle differences seem absurd, but are definitively not something of the past. Also in our contemporary societies that call themselves democratic and where often the bosses are addressed by their first name, we can see the influence of social hierarchy on manners. How many employees laugh harder at the silly joke of their bosses than of their colleagues? How easily they take the side of their boss, even if the colleague is right. Struggles for status symbols are fought in organisations even today – over the size of the office or the number of windows at the workplace, for instance. Hierarchical positions are clearly visible in the sphere and form of conversations.

C'est le ton qui fait la musique! The relation between people determines the tone of their conversation, but at the same time the inverse is true. The relation between strangers can be deduced from the nature and tone of their interaction. 'Come here' indicates quite a different relationship than the request 'Could you be so kind to come over for a moment?' If the social distance between both interlocutors is too wide, communication can become impossible. Sometimes such an inequality can be forgotten for a moment, but not for long. In a concentration camp, the prisoners are not spoken to; they are 'Untermenschen', not human. George Semprun forgets this for a moment when he is marching back to Buchenwald. He becomes impressed by the beauty of a tree covered with snow. He walks to this tree, leaving the path. 'Suddenly next to me is an SS-officer. He asked me what I was doing there. And without realising that he had directed his pistol at me, I answered: 'This tree is beautiful, don't you think?', like the SS-officer was a normal person. Very surprised, he let his gun down and looked at the tree. And before he became an SS-officer again and started to shout, it seemed for a moment that we were able to communicate.'[4]

Tact and presentation of self   Semprun's story illustrates that in a conversation, in spite of existing positions and pressure of the environment, the relation between interlocutors is not permanently fixed. Relations can change. Even in an unequal situation, the balance can change in the opposite direction. A conversation is like a traditional dance, say a waltz, in which the leading person depends on the partner, and has to anticipate and to readjust. This demands a continuous scanning of each position. Nobody has explained better how this process of coping and adjusting occurs than Irving Goffman. His point of departure is the existence of two basic human needs: on the one hand, the will to be a free and autonomous human being; on the other hand, the need to be recognised and respected by others. Those needs, which can sometimes clash with each other, demand an active attitude in dealing with people. Two important strategies are available: tact and presentation of self.

Tact is more than politeness or courtesy; it is basically respect for the other. Tact knows two forms. The first is positive, recognises the other, shows appreciation of the other, and recognises his or her value. Giving compliments and praising the other's performance empowers the other, increasing their self-confidence – indispensable in the education and base for growing as a healthy self-confident person. Positive feedback is the oil of human relations. But tact knows also a negative form: 'face work', in Gofmann´s words. This means all efforts to prevent loss of face by the partner in the conversation. A perfect example given is of the Dutch Queen Wilhelmina who imitated the faux pas of her guest, the South African President Kruger, during a banquet, by drinking water from a finger bowl instead of the water glass. Most of the time tact is more subtle. Listen to the following dialogue between two colleagues. 'A' says, 'What is your opinion of my report?' 'B' answers: 'Very interesting, but it could use some polishing.' Actually, the colleague thinks that it is a bad report, but he tries not to hurt the feelings of the writer. Tact involves empathising with others and avoiding things that threaten them, things that can offend them or hurt their feelings.

In summary, tact is the preoccupation with the other's face. This implies that self-presentation is more preoccupied with the self-image. What is the impression I make on the other? Answering this question requires self-monitoring. Indeed, during a meeting, people are concerned with questions like 'How is my hair; is my dress proper? Should I meet the other's eyes now or look away?' The participants also consider the physical space between them. 'A' steps back when 'B' enters the private personal space. The concern with a positive impression during a meeting is mostly realised on an unconscious level. Being tactful requires subtle modifications of verbal and non-verbal activities to signal awareness of each other's feelings, e.g., becoming more indirect when talking about uncomfortable topics, making criticisms in a pleasant tone of voice, etc.

How difficult it is to maintain the balance between the defence of a person's autonomy, on the one hand, and respect for the other, in turn, is illustrated by the difficult interaction between Moroccan immigrant youngsters and Dutch-born adults, which has become a much-debated social problem in The Netherlands.[5] These boys, from families of Moroccan immigrants who came to The Netherlands from the 1960s onward, often attract media attention by aggressiveness to neighbours and macho behaviour vis-à-vis women. The easy and commonly-accepted explanation for this type of behaviour is 'their cultural background'. No doubt, their socialisation in families coming from a non-industrialised society is an explicatory factor, but it's only a small part of the story. Studies show that crucial here is the clash between their need for respect on the one hand and recognition on the other – the marginalisation of these boys in Dutch society. Their self-esteem is under fire from all sides: police, neighbours and teachers. Giving and receiving respect are out of balance. How those adolescents give and demand respect is greatly situation-dependent. In the family context, respect for authority, namely the father, is very much emphasised, but in the peer group self-autonomy scores higher. A young man's honour can easily be offended by someone belittling or challenging him. Anyone in this subculture who loses face is apt to react with aggressiveness. Like Omar explains: 'We live in the kind of place where if someone 'disses' you and you don't do anything back, you are finished. For the rest of your life everyone just thinks you are a sissy and that's that. But if you hit them and you do stupid things, that is that, and then you are the hero.'[6] Self-esteem and recognition by others normally go together; problems arise when, as in this case, assertiveness and the preoccupation with self-image take the upper hand.[7]

Sociologists[8] have made clear that we cannot isolate those incidents of immigrant aggression from cultural change at a more global level. Assertiveness is not only a characteristic of immigrant youth subculture; individuals in general have become more autonomous and their self-esteem has grown. Equality has become the norm in interpersonal interaction. At the same time, there is also greater vulnerability to anything that might offend an individual's self-respect. An assertive lifestyle has become a dominant characteristic of our society. At the same time, the decline of traditional relations of authority has resulted in greater emphasis being placed on social norms and self-control. Equals are respected in their autonomy, but that is far less the case for people that are not viewed as equals. In Western democracies, people are so focused on their own rights and their own place in a minority of women, gays, handicapped, or blacks such that they almost forget that presentation of self and assertiveness are impossible without recognition of the rights of others.

Tact and presentation of self are culturally determined, which means that how they are used varies between groups. When a domestic helper in Lombok (Indonesia) informs her white employer with a big smile that she cannot come to work because her child has passed away, that is a consequence of tact or care for the employer's feelings. The basic idea of Anglo-American tact is to prevent as much as possible that the partner in conversation lose face, and is supported in their self-esteem by positive feedback. The Dutch typically tend to avoid loss of face. Positive feedback is perceived by most Dutch people as exaggeration or even a lie. However, to be respected and recognised is a basic and general human need. Tact and self-presentation are basic mechanisms to construct and maintain human relationships.

The emphasis on the relational aspect of communication will not deny the existence of content, central in good or bad news meetings and crucial for professionals. However, neglect of the relation causes much miscommunication. If the sender gives the receiver the impression that the latter is not respected, is despised, or that the first will dominate without respect for the autonomy of the other, then the receiver is personally touched and will assume an attitude of combat or at least defence. However, often the solution for this kind of poor communication is sought at the level of content and not of the relation. When one colleague reproaches another with 'How can you propose such a stupid plan!', the other will become angry and feel hurt. But what can he or she do? Mostly the reaction is to defend the proposal with more force in order to save one's own face. As we will see in Chapter 6, only meta-communication – talking about the way people is communicating – can solve this lack of real communication.

Constructing identities   Relations are more than just an aspect of communication. As social beings, we become ourselves in communicating with others. The images of self depend on others. What it means to be a woman or a man, to be an Englishman or a Muslim, are not decided by individuals, but by society. Presentation of self, the self-image and recognition and evaluation by the social environment determine together a person's identity. In the interaction – being perceived and recognised by others – we become ourselves. I will illustrate this with some examples, starting with some negative ones.

The famous Dutch football player Ruud Gullit, born and brought up in Amsterdam, only realised himself to be a 'Surinamese' after a remark by an angry policeman. The sociologist Stuart Hall, born in Jamaica, only became in the UK a 'black Caribbean'. As a scientist, he is more explicit about his experience than Gullit, but the experience is based on the same precept; categories used by others construct your identity. When Hall is back home for a short family visit, his own mother says:

'I hope they do not think there that you are one of those immigrants.' And writes Hall: 'Of course, at that moment I realised for the first time to be an immigrant.'[9] In the same essay, he explains that his own sense of identity has always been dependent on difference, in his case with the white British population. Immigrants and refugees are continually confronted with the tendency to make them strangers, i.e. to see them as different from the majority. 'Your English is excellent.' 'Yes, I am born here.' Perhaps the remark was meant to be a compliment, but it becomes a de facto way to emphasise the differences between both. Of course, identities exist because of differences with others. These can be race, colour, age, language, gender, etc. In gender training, it has become a popular tool to ask the participants when they became first became aware of being a boy or girl. Most answers indeed connote something dramatic. The North American feminist Judith Butler did research on the influence of speech on gender identities – the ways of becoming and being a woman or a man. It is not just one remark, however denigrating this may be, like the remark of a male colleague: 'Look, you (women) don't understand. I will explain this.' It is the continuous repetition of these kind of remarks that will influence the self-perception of men and women.

Luckily, the influence of partners in conversation on social identities is not only negative. Ego can be influenced in a positive way by compliments, acknowledgement, declaration of love, or positive feedback in the private sphere. More official forms of identity construction are 'singing one's praise', rendering homage to someone celebrating a jubilee, assigning someone a decoration, consecrating a priest or bishop, taking the oath during naturalisation, knighting a person or giving a doctorate for the sake of honour – or even winning a TV contest such as Idols.

In spite of its popularity in the social sciences, identity is not an easy or clear concept.[10] Psychoanalysis has taught us that identity does not imply a real authentic ego, i.e. a nucleus of the person that remains after digging through all superficial layers – 'the real me'. We cannot speak about a stable self, remaining the same over time. Even our self-consciousness changes all the time. Identity is historically situated, depending on the time and place and, although also objective, it is a construction with two dimensions: it is a social position, with its evaluation given by others and, at the same time, a self-image, in accordance with the first or in opposition. Identity is always related to the social position a person occupies in the social field. The differences with other positions can be positive or negative. In the first case, as seen in Chapter 1, we talk about distinction; in the second case – a negative difference – we speak about stigmatisation. The construction of social identity in the sense of marking differences with others is mostly based on clear and visible differences like skin colour, accent or sexual differences. This marker becomes a symbol for a cluster of real and/or supposed properties. The name 'immigrant' has become a stigmatising identity, a negative evaluation of difference. Expressions like 'intellectual' or 'stud' are titles of distinction, although quite different in tone.

Identity is not thinkable without identification, an active appropriation of an image. People appropriate the images they receive from their social environment; they become the image the social mirror presents them. That is obvious in cases where the images are positive. It is more difficult to understand why people identify with images that are negative: Negro, housewife, welfare recipient. Only symbolic violence active in hierarchical societies explains why people accept their low, subordinate positions. This means that victims declare themselves guilty for their own destiny. 'If I had studied better at school, then I would not be a drug dealer,' as a young slum dweller in Porto Alegre once told me, not long before he was killed in a gunfight with the local police. He had his inferior social position interiorised and accepted as self-evident. Common sense knows for sure that 'Who has been born to be a dime never will become a quarter.' Luckily, social positions are not so fixed as in traditional societies, but the negative side of this change is that more is demanded from people in order to situate themselves. Still, a 'sense of place' is quite common; people know unconsciously what is 'normal' in their position – as well as what is unthinkable – and will adapt to that.

Identities are human-made, not directly a consequence of giving names in a private conversation, but the result of categorisation by authorised speakers like politicians and journalists who invent them and legitimise them. Individuals are categorised and identified as' Australian', 'married', 'immigrants', and 'Muslims'. Those basic categories are used to place people

and to give them a position. The social differences relat[e]
these positions are used to include or exclude people. Tho[se]
names are like passports – those official documents that determine people's nationality or its lack, and their exclusion from
the nation as illegal. Identity and social position are in this
respect different expressions for the same phenomenon. The
relations between people in social space can be, at a horizontal
level, intimate or distant and, at a vertical level, active or passive, influencing or following. In a recent conversation, a Brazilian university professor complained about the difficulty of
addressing his students – how to avoid being too distant without becoming too intimate, how to avoid superiority while
maintaining the natural hierarchy between a professor and a
student. In Portuguese ways of addressing a person, a choice
can be made between three forms: *tu*, *voce*, *senhor(a)*, from more
intimate to more distant. But even in English you can vary in
this respect through intonation and context. Besides distance,
power differences are equally important in conversations. I will
elaborate on the influence of power using the role of language
in conversations.

Differences in power   Dutch TV organises every year a
'Great Dictation' of the Dutch language. Public personalities
compete with unknown individuals from The Netherlands and
Belgium for the honour of writing as correctly as possible without errors in orthography. This TV 'happening' fortifies the impression that the national language is like a treasure, accessible
for all speakers in an equal way. However, this is wrong. The
competence in a language does not depend on spelling correctly. It is not the technical command of a language (choice of
words, spelling or grammar) but the social and cultural capital,
i.e. the position of the speaker, which decides on the status of
his language. Decisive is the social status and its recognition of
the speakers or writers. The fact that President Bush's English is
far from correct does not matter. He is not speaking as a private
person but as a representative of the most powerful nation on
this earth. It is possible to generalise this idea. A speaker can
influence others' behaviour more if he or she has been mandat-
ed and speaks as a representative of a group or institution. Officials always have a mandate: they speak in the Queen's name,

...ie name of the law, or they confirm a mar-
...of the church. The effect of their speech is
...authority and status. Even a stutterer such as the
...or Claudius could speak effectively, because he

...s are not only representatives of a group or institu-
...hey also speak an official language. They speak in The
Netherlands what is generally called 'civilized Dutch', the standard language. This name already implies that other sociolects
and dialects are not civilised. Prince Carnival can speak the local
dialect of Maastricht, Holland's most southern city. However,
the Prince of Orange will never do that, even less he will speak
the popular variations of Dutch. Language is a clear marker of a
person's social position. It indicates if we belong to the cultural
elite, a group that prefers euphemistic use of language, or if we
belong to the traditional middle class with an exaggerated concern with correct use of the language, or to the working class,
which likes to call things by their name. Language also guides
the perception people have of others. Linguists have established
a clear relation between someone's appreciation and his language. Without taking into account the content, a speaker who
uses a language with high status is more readily considered to
be competent and higher valued. [11]

Because of the social differences between several kinds of
speech, it is not enough to learn a new language before departing to another country. Whose language should we learn? The
language of the local elite or the common man? In a country
like Brazil, an abyss separates both kinds of languages. The
structure of Portuguese is relatively simple, but the elite have
the use of language refined and cultivated in such a way that
correct writing and speech have become a marker of high social
capital. The specialists in grammar can enjoy disputes on
accents, but for the majority of the population, its correct use is
an illusion. In this way, language helps to maintain distances in
power.

Power is used in speech not only by the kind of language
used, but also by the way people speak. In Western democracies, patriarchal authority is not popular and is outdated. Contemporary leadership is based on emotional tact and skills
learned in the practice. [12] But even the captain of industry uses,

besides his experience and emotional skills, his status. Opening a meeting in an organisation is not everyone's prerogative, even not in a democratic organisation. Opening is the chairperson's privilege. Other people present can ask to start the meeting, but not to open it. In a personal conversation in everyday life, power is executed by controlling or even monopolising the time of speech. It is possible to prevent the other person from finishing his/ her speech or to silence by interrupting. Communicative competence is also the art to be heard - forcing the others to listen, preferably without the others noticing it as forcing.

Transforming power   In human interaction, influencing, and thus power, is always at stake, even if we look at it from a psychological perspective. Psychologists talk about the appealing aspect of conversations. This is clear in the case of direct requests like: 'Please, close the window.' However, it is also present in messages like: 'It is the market that will end inequalities between nations.' This is an example of an ideological message shaped by specific interest. Use of power is mostly a lot more subtle. I have mentioned already the symbolic violence allowing others to name and to define reality and everyone's position in it, as in this phrase: 'You immigrants are a social problem!' However, is power necessarily negative? Does it always aim at domination and inequality?

Research by feminists has shown that power can be used in a positive way without oppression. Besides the power of the patriarch, other forms of power exist that are aimed at the growth of others – not power *over* but power *to*, e.g. power that stimulates the autonomy and capacities of employees, students or children – the kind of power that an educator like Socrates was using, setting the other free. Power, knowledge and competences are not used to impress the other or to yield, but to empower the others by increasing their self-esteem.[13] Defending here the need to scan power relations in communication is not, because I believe that self-interest is the main motivator for people. Compassion, love, solidarity are other motivators equally possible. Educators, parents, political and social mobilizers can do their job successfully only if they aim at the empowerment of their target group. This is not an easy job. Many persons ignore their own power, resources or capital We can identify four forms. First there is material capital, i.e. one's income and possessions. Second, there is social power, like the family (influential or humble) you have been born into, origin, and the relations a person can mobilize. Third is cultural, e.g. the formal education one has received, the diplomas one has earned, and the languages a person can speak. Last but not least is the symbolic and psychological capital – the self-confidence of a person, the charm or charisma recognized by others. Only if recognised does it turn into power. The worst dimension of poverty is the lack of self-confidence and the doubt of one's own power.

Even if we try to aim at the empowerment of the other, this is not self-evident. Often we have to convince the other party of our positive intentions. The past history of a group can interfere very negatively. When immigrants of ex-colonies and indigenous British or Dutch meet each other, the colonial past of both groups plays a role, even in the background. There is always the possibility of suspicion of the white person wanting to repeat colonial attitudes. This doubt and suspicion should be neutralised before a conversation between equals becomes possible. The same mechanisms are at stake when you work as a white person in Africa. You should first convince your African colleagues that you are not a neo-colonial. Likewise, you have to convince your feminist friends that you are not a 'male chauvinist pig' before being accepted as an emancipated male.

Communication and corporality   The attention given until now as to the role of language in communication does not imply that words are the central elements here. All specialists agree that the role of non-verbal aspects is more important. [14] Communication is basically a corporal happening. The use of Internet seems to argue in favour of the old Cartesian thesis of body and soul division. New age defends similar positions – the possibility of communication without a body. For sure, we humans are able to think, but we are not spirits. No need to start here a philosophical debate; it is enough to observe human interaction to become aware of the crucial role of body language. The moment that public opinion became conscious of the importance of non-verbal communication was during the TV-debate between Richard Nixon and John Kennedy. Kennedy, more relaxed than his tired opponent, won the preference of the TV audience. However, the radio audience, only listening, voted for Nixon's performance as the more convincing.

Body language can be sub-divided into many aspects. We only analyse some elements here to show the importance of this aspect in communication. First are the movements of the arms and hands, very important in transmitting the emotional load of the message, depending on the group's introvert or extrovert character. A specific aspect is the *gestures* researched by Desmond Morris in various Mediterranean countries. He shows how the same gesture can mean quite different things. For instance, the gesture made by putting the finger tops together in a circle. Its significance can vary according to the various regions where the users live. In Southern Italy, it means precision and is a request for more clarity. In Greece and Turkey, it predominantly means appreciation of the precision and, therefore, means that something is good. In Spain, the gesture connotes many unities together and means plenty. In France, this gesture refers to the sphincter and means fear (when it is often difficult to control bowel movements). Another example is nodding with the head (throwing one's head backwards). In Turkey it means no; in Tunisia it is used to indicate you over there . Those variations do not coincide with national frontiers; they vary with regions, going back in some cases probably to Grecian immigration in ancient Italy!

Body language goes further and knows many unconscious and non-intentional dimensions. An example is the physical *distance* people maintain from each other in a face-to-face situation in which they feel comfortable. Among Creole (Black) Surinamese, this distance is on average a lot smaller then the norm among native Dutch. Research in Amsterdam proved that Surinamese appreciate close contact more positively than most Dutch. The majority of the Dutch readily experience close co-presence as an intrusion of their own personal space. Similar mechanisms explain communication problems between white police officers and black Surinamese, the latter of which are mostly cooperative when interrogated by the police. Why then are there more problems with this category during detention? The explanation was found in the non-verbal communication of the arrested Surinamese by the white Dutch policeman. The normal style of Surinamese communication implies a lot of smiling, a slow pattern of response, many gestures and touching of one's own body. For the Dutch cops, those gestures meant that these suspects did not feel at ease and was, for them, an indication that they were guilty.[15]

The *look or gaze* is another important non-verbal way of communicating. A glance and a gaze are quite different forms of interaction. A colleague told me how he had learned from his mother in the Caribbean island of Curacao to look away when his mother corrected him. His Surinamese grandmother became angry by this same behaviour! Generally speaking, any eye contact between people for more than eight seconds causes people to wonder what is going on? It is perceived as aggressive or seen as a wish to become intimate. Experiments have demonstrated that a longer look indeed implies domination. The not-dominant partner in the conversation looks away. Even the size of the pupil can influence the communication. Bigger pupils make a face more sympathetic. Merchants in the Middle East seem to be able to check the size of their customers' pupils in order to measure their interest in the merchandise. 'Eyes compel' is a Dutch expression. For the same reason, people in the Middle East and Latin America look for protection against the evil (i.e. jealous) eye. Control of another's look is an important aspect of scanning in a face-to-face meeting. More expressive still is the overall expression of someone's face: smile, fear, surprise, hatred, or happiness.

Body posture is another way to communicate. A person can make him or herself small and invisible or be very present , and that is not dependent on the size of the person's body. People tend during a meeting to assume the same postures, like crossing their arms, when they agree with each other. If they disagree or do not like each other, they tend to turn away. Officials of the Dutch immigration services told me once how irritated they could become by the way African asylum seekers sat down limp and lax in their chairs during the interviews. They interpreted this posture as a lack of interest or as rejection.

Touching is the most corporal form of communication. It can be quite embarrassing if your white extended hand is not accepted by a female in a country like Yemen. But in a lot of places, touching between men and women is taboo, also between strangers. In Nepal, you greet with a bow, placing both hands palms together in front of your breast. In all societies, touching is governed by many implicit rules. Who may touch where and in what circumstances? It is virtually impossible to know. However, foreigners are seldom expected to know; most locals realise that foreigners will behave oddly and that they have their funny ways, as is already recognised from film or TV. Kissing is one of the most intimate forms of touching. You don't kiss the queen, of course, because she needs distance from her followers.

Finally is *facial expression*. The face is the dominant site of non-verbal communication. Intentions and emotions are conveyed by expressions such as smiles or frowns that, used consciously or unconsciously, betray states of mind. The differences in expressions across cultures first received a lot of attention, starting with Darwin's hypothesis that repression of all outward signs softens our emotions, while the stimulation of an emotion tends to arouse it – meaning that emotions as consequence of human intervention are cultural. Later scientists tended to place emphasis on the innate character of emotions and their expressions. Paul Ekman and others selected photographs of specific emotional facial expressions that, by people from different cultures, were decoded in the same way. Ekman later came to the conclusion that, to a large extent, differences exist between groups in the language they use to name emotions, the categories used to indicate emotions. Lately, consensus seems to dictate that both theses might be true. On the one hand, there is a similarity between men and primates in expressing their emotions; on the other hand, human individuals and groups can manipulate their emotions and expressions in very different ways.

Women and men   Varieties in the repertoire of communication not only depend on ethnic, class or regional differences. Gender is everywhere – a very influential factor in communication, and especially in the communication between men and women. The way most men tend to communicate differs substantially from the female way. Men are more inclined to interrupt the other party than women, who tend to follow more the pace of the conversation. Women look more after solidarity than status. They give more compliments; they excuse themselves quicker than most men do and are less direct then men – a conversation style that is detrimental for women because it causes (for most men) an impression of insecurity. How do we explain these differences? It is certainly not because women follow the advice books of either traditional or more modern times as to how to deal with men. The causes can be found at the heart of our societies, as Bourdieu explains.[16]

For Bourdieu, society functions as big symbolic machinery, legitimating the male dominance as the foundation of the social order. The biological difference between men and women becomes a legitimisation of unequal positions for both sexes on all levels, not only in work and responsibilities, but also in the distribution of resources, time and opportunities. That self-evident order is time and time again appropriated by individual men and women and translated into typical male and female behaviour. This order is not a conscious construction but a consequence of male and female body language, an incorporation of unequal perception of the world. Our behaviour in relation to the opposite sex has become a natural function of our education that taught us to react in a way that is typical for a girl or a boy. How arbitrary this behaviour is, as one notices when later in life a person discovers that he or she prefers people from his/her own sex. In a similar way, although less dramatic, we can discover the arbitrariness of those differences in a not familiar situation. The alternative tourist guide explains this by instructing the correct ways for girls and boys to take a dip on the Cariocan beach in Brazil.[17] Women should walk slowly to the shoreline, continuously adjusting the bottom of their *tanga (bikini bottom)*, and enter the sea by first putting their bottom in the water. Men, on the contrary, will run to the sea and dive in the water. After the dip, again a different behaviour, the men will never sit on a towel; that is for women and children only. A male Carioca will sit on the sand. The guide gives many more rules that differ according to gender. A visit to Ipanema or Copacabana will convince you that, indeed, most men and women in Rio show a gender-specific behaviour. The rules, regardless of how exaggerated they seem to be, are followed.

Similar differences can be found in the way men and women in North Africa use space. Summarizing a research done in a small Algerian town, we can say that men communicate by their body posture that they are big and broad, while women give the impression of being small and short. Men sit higher and take more space by putting their arms and legs further from their rump; they stand more erect, and this impression is fortified by clothing and other attributes. The only women that can behave similarly to men are prostitutes. They can challenge the male domination because they are outcast and without real honour![18]

Non-verbal communication expresses people's attitude and, at the same time, gives it form. This is also valid in situations of change. A new mentality or a new attitude must become visible in a different body posture. The Chilean father who teaches his son to look up to him when speaking with his father has understood that well. He was educated with the Indian tradition of casting down your eyes when talking with authorities. A new sense of self-confidence demands another behaviour and posture.

Scanning as process   The main objective of this chapter is to explain what personal communication is. We have already dealt with the essential elements needed to understand its essence, such as positioning, relationships, tact, self-presentation, power and non-verbal communication. Finalizing this chapter, we will review those elements, but for now let's focus on process. To understand better the dynamics of personal communication, some new concepts will be introduced: situation, context, repertory, strategies, turn-taking, code-switching and genres. These concepts offer an opportunity to see the differences and similarities between the proposed scan model and other approaches to communication.

Situation   An acquaintance working in the selection of personnel told me once how she had felt embarrassed during an interview with an Iranian young man. He had posed many questions about the position of women in Dutch society – questions that for her seemed to be too personal and not relevant to the situation. She could not imagine that the boy was really interested in this topic. Clearly, both parties interpreted the situation quite differently. Indeed, every form of conversation has its own rule and form; administration of justice is quite different from courting a lady, a confession in the church, a sales talk, or a lecture. Although all are forms of meetings, they each involve specific patterns of behaviour that are supposed to be known. This is, of course, not always the case. Lack of understanding of cultural specificity can interfere with communication. For example, a typical Dutch business lunch with only bread is an affront for most international guests. Goffman has made an interesting distinction between focused and unfocused meetings. By the latter, he implies the type of situation in which people are face-to-face, seeing one another, but there is no direct interaction. This is mostly the case in large gatherings such as theatre audiences, parties or groups of people on a street. On the streets or public transport of major cities, people employ civilised inattention. This means that, by looking away and avoiding contact, they do not bother others. Focused interaction occurs when individuals directly attend to what others say or do. A unit of focused interaction is called an 'encounter'. Small talk, formal meetings, face-to-face contacts (with teachers, shopkeepers, and waiters) are examples of encounters. They always start with an opening and are finished with a short ritual, e.g. a greeting and then a closing action. In general, framing is needed – an understanding of the rules that are specific to each kind of meeting and which sustain the ontological security in the enactment of daily routines. A person knows, for instance, that what is allowed in a dating situation is not permitted during a funeral.

Context   The situation of a meeting differs from its context, with includes a lot more. Specialists in communication often use the expression 'to contextualise a message'. This means that the comprehension of a message supposes the knowledge of what has *not* been said but has been implied. A question such as 'What did you do yesterday?' should lead to a description of all activities that you did yesterday. When it is a colleague who is asking that, you know that it is enough to tell what you did last night after work. Successful communication demands the capacity to situate the other as member of a group, class or ethnic group – a central activity of scanning.

   Context is also used to indicate differences between cultures – between high- and low-context cultures. Edward Hall made this distinction for the first time, opposing in this way two forms of communicating. The first is rather implicit, with a strong accent on body language. The place and the situation of the meeting give more information about its meaning than the words spoken. The other form needs more words and verbal explanation, is explicit, and doesn't trust the capacity of interpretation of the other party. In this case, a refusal is expressed straight or even bluntly. In the first case, the refusal is expressed indirectly without using expressions like 'no'. Hall has defined the USA and Germany as low-context cultures, and China and Japan as high-context cultures. This distinction has become popular among trainers involved in intercultural communication, although they sometimes forget that Hall has emphasised that the opposition is relative. It is not a question of one or the other, but of less or more. We could say that each personal communication depends basically on the context – that it is highly contextual. Good friends need only half a word to understand each other, even in The Netherlands or United Kingdom, known to be low-context countries.

Meeting's structure   Meetings are normally structured according to starting a conversation, finishing it and turn-taking. Again, the start of a meeting demands a lot of tact, especially with unfamiliar people. Will I present myself first or can I immediately enter into the business at hand? How shall I present myself? On a first-name basis or by using my family name …and with titles or not? Would titles be perceived as imposing and ostentatious or as useful information? In The Netherlands, mentioning your academic titles is not the norm. At the university of Sanaa, Yemen's capital, every time someone is addressed during a discussion, his/her titles are mentioned. It seems not very efficient, but it is a means of recognition.

In talking with 'strangers', let us not forget the problem of first impressions, often based on stereotyping, as we have seen in Chapter 1. The first impression you get from someone is, to a large extent, determined by your own positive or negative emotions. Without being aware, you can be influenced by negative feelings about another person who happened to be similar.[19] As a trainer, I once had a problem with one of the participants in building a positive understanding. In spite of all efforts, I did not succeed. At the end of the training, she finally told me the reason: I reminded her of her father with whom she had a conflicting relation.

According to Goffman, meetings are characterized by markers: openings and endings. Take a reception, for instance, where a businessman is busy with networking. He walks from one small group to another, introducing himself every time and probably also closing the meeting with a sentence like, 'Okay, I must go on'. Closing a meeting can happen in a more complicated way, such as with funeral rituals. In the Roman Catholic version, the last word of closure is all the time postponed by another ritual or prayer until the final praying of 'Our Father who art in heaven'. Markers are especially important in ambivalent situations like a gynaecological examinations by a male physician. In such cases, special measures are taken, such as change of place (behind a curtain) and position (presence of a nurse), to exclude ambivalence.[20]

Turn-taking   Interrupting the other party in a meeting and taking over is another important structuring element. Who can be interrupted? You don't interrupt the word of a queen, for example. When does the other take a turn? In French and Latin American conversation styles, turn-taking is quick and simultaneous – no need to let the other finish the sentence first. A Dutch development worker transferred with his work from Peru to Tanzania. In Tanzania, he took turns over quickly, in the way he had become accustomed, without realising that he was killing the conversation. Unbeknownst to him, Tanzanians need more time to take over a conversation than is customary in Latin America. Waiting for your turn often implies, at least in Latin America, that you are uninterested, lazy or even stupid. In Tanzania, as well as many other countries, people communicate in another rhythm.

Linguists have tried to understand the dynamics of turn-taking. To do so, they make the distinction between acts of speech, consequences of an initiative and of reactions. Requests, questions and commands are examples of the first kind. Acceptance and answering are examples of the second kind. The psychologist Leary links this pattern of interaction with the two dimensions that we discussed before. In his vision, each communicative action causes a reaction. He made an inventory of

the global possibilities by using the two basic α
communication: distance and power. Distance, for exan
vary from working together – being near until being in opp
tion and aloof. Power can vary from being active, such as taking
initiatives until following or resigning one's self. If one party
shows cooperative behaviour, the other will, most of the time,
adopt the same attitude, while opposition evokes mostly action
against the grain.

In a meeting, the positions of the interlocutors are not
fixed, but can change all the time. The initiative is not automatically with the boss; the employee can take it over, even if the
boss is correcting him or her. But the context, the objective positions of both parties, will not change that easily. Superiors
always have more resources to use power. However, we have
seen that the inferior also has power. On the other axis of distance or affection, changes can also occur. An attitude of opposition can change into cooperation. And the opposite can occur;
cooperation can change into opposition because one of the parties has the impression of being threatened and losing face.
Continuously, it is necessary to check the reactions of the interlocutors and to adapt the communication process.

Of course turn-taking is more formal in institutional settings such as an interview or courts of law. Institutional interaction is systematically asymmetrical. The institutional agents
have the power to define the position of the interviewee by
manipulating categories and defining the problem. A study of
the interviews held in the National Directory of Migrations in
Buenos Aires made clear how this functioned in practice. The
interviews started with questions as to where the person came
from and what was his/her work, looking for the categories that
would make it easy to identify the group to which the person
belonged. This stimulated the other party to self-categorisa-
tion. Stereotyping was always near.[21]

Code-switching   In the context of intercultural communication, switching of linguistic codes is also very important for the
dynamics of the conversation. Code-switching can assume a
simple form, e.g. using words from two different languages in
one sentence, to complex forms, in which people use two different types of grammar in one sentence. It can mean changing

another or into another sociolect. The ...ing is often viewed negatively by mono-...speakers alike. It is often considered a low-...correct, poor language, or a result of incom-...ie two languages. However, the complexity of ...ode-switching requires that the speakers have knowledge of the grammars of both languages, ...owledge of how those grammars map onto one anou... ...s proficient bilinguals favour single-word and tag switches, while more proficient bilinguals utilise switched codes at the phrase and clause level as well. Intra-sentential code-switching proficiency requires an adult command of both languages, and it seems that it supposes more cultural competence than most mono-linguistic speakers dispose of. The problem with code-switching is that, in most cases, the languages involved don't have the same prestige. On Curacao island, for instance, Dutch as the official language in the educational system has a higher status then the local language, 'Papiamento', even though for the people of this island this language is essential for their identity. It is this in-equal position that determines code-switching and the relations between users of those languages. Members of minorities can, via the use of certain words and style, make clear to a stranger what their mother tongue is and, in this way, propose an identity. Depending on the reaction of the other can he/she change the code to be used or, the opposite, enlarge the distance with the other. Code-switching can also become very complex. During research in New York, a second-generation Haitian told the following: 'When I am at school and I sit with my black friends and sometimes I'm ashamed to say this, but my accent changes. I learn all the words; I switch. Well, when I'm with my black friends, I say I'm black – black American. When I'm with my Haitian-American friends, I say I'm Haitian.' [22]

Dutch public opinion and politicians make a big issue about the lack of domination of the national language by the first generation of immigrants; they forget that the second generation is becoming 'skilled cultural navigators with a sophisticated ability to manoeuvre between different social worlds.' [23] This quote by Roger Ballard refers to second-generation Asians in the UK, but we can generalise this image. In The Netherlands we find similar abilities among second-generation Moroccans, Turks, and Surinamese. Someone who dominates Dutch and Turkish can speak with friends a local dialect, mixed with Turkish elements. The same speaker can use this local dialect with Dutch fiends in a sport club, and Standard Dutch at the same time. He or she is able to speak Turkish mixed with Dutch elements in a Turkish social network, and pure Turkish with older relatives.[24] This person demonstrates a cultural competence that is rare among the majority of the Dutch!

Genres A final element important to understanding the dynamics of a personal meeting is genre or style. This concept is borrowed from literature studies where it refers to the different styles used to write texts. The distinctions made in the genres depend on the intention of the analysis. The same applies to speech. Sermons, consultations, pleas, interviews, sketches, stories and jokes each have their own rules of the game. Of course genre is linked with the situation, but genre is preoccupied overall with form and style, although those can change through artistic innovation. It is impossible to explain here the specific aspects of each genre for the communication process. Perhaps it is enough to illustrate the importance of genre by elaborating upon the example of humour and joking.

There's no doubt that humour is very much influenced by cultural differences. Experts in intercultural communication defend the thesis that understanding of humour of another culture is a pathway to intercultural competence.[25] Humour itself is practiced in many forms, such as slapstick, cabaret, stand-up comedy, clowns, TV satire, sitcoms, cartoons, and, of course, jokes. Recently, a Dutch scholar dedicated an academic thesis to jokes in Dutch society. I will summarise the interesting results here, because it proves once again how cultural products are not only determined by national culture but also by other variables, such as gender and social class. Jokes are a sub-genre of humour different from other forms such as irony and understatement. Telling a joke effectively demands a special competence that you have to learn, and not everyone is able to do so. Character introduction, timing, clues, the surprising shift in meaning at the right moment – all intended to make the audience laugh – are some of its essential elements. However, the research showed that this competence is not equally distributed among the population, nor the interest or acceptance. The real joke-teller is characterised by an extensive and exuberant style of storytelling – imitating voices and accents and gesticulating expressively. This is one of the reasons that not everyone is fond of this competence. When someone starts telling jokes, the nature of the conversation changes radically. The joker takes the conversation over. He (almost exclusively men) monopolises speech and challenges others, as a way of being funnier. This behaviour fits more in the dominant male communication style. Women prefer the opposite. They are more concerned about constructing and maintaining good relations.

Besides gender, class – more precisely the level of education – is a factor explaining love of or disgust of joke-telling. Kuipers' research demonstrates that in The Netherlands, two different types of humour exist: a popular type versus an elitist type. The first kind puts emphasis on the social character of humour: telling jokes is a social happening, creating a positive ambiance, with performance being more important than content; but hurting people's feelings should be avoided. The elitist style is the opposite: content is more important, i.e. intellect, spirit, wit and creativity. This kind of humour is not concerned with sociability, and can stimulate and even provoke. Joke versus wit! The first style is correlated with working or lower middle-class culture, the second with academic or similar educational level. We may conclude that typical Dutch humour does not exist. At least in this case, no direct link between jokes and national culture exists. It is not clear if it is possible to generalise those findings, but the difference between Benny Hill and Monty Python suggest that class, also in the UK, can play a role in the appreciation of humour.

Why scanning?   Hopefully, the critical reader of this book is convinced by now that scanning during meetings makes sense. However, you might wonder, why the emphasis on relations, tact and concern for the other's feelings? Is this approach really new? How was this done before? Communication can be effective without respect and or tact in hierarchical situations in which the other is powerless, but this situation is not common. In the last decades, ongoing social change has also affected the forms of interaction. In his book, *The Lonely Crowd* (1956), David Riesman was one of the first to describe this change. He distinguishes three broad phases in the history of communication. The first is the communication directed by tradition. In traditional societies, functions and roles were fixed and everyone knew what to do and what to avoid. A fisherman or blacksmith occupied a clear position and was treated accordingly. In modern times, after the Renaissance, things changed. A new kind of person emerged – inner-directed. A person who was guided y his/her conscience like an internalised compass, which was always followed even against the pressure of the social environment. The prototype of this posture is Martin Luther standing before the Emperor and declaring, 'Here I stand and I cannot do otherwise.' Following one's own conscience is the ultimate norm. The third type is typical for the post-modern epoch: an outer-directed human being, following the others and his/her social environment. One's own conscience is no longer functioning like a compass. People follow this orientation toward others as if radar scanning their surroundings. Youngsters react continually on signals from their direct environment and adapt their behaviour accordingly. They conform their actions in accordance with people from the same age and group. Maybe Riesman is somewhat too pessimistic but his prophetic vision has anticipated clearly the growing importance of psychology in contemporary society.

Some years ago, Eva Illouz convincingly analysed how in the post-modern society, in both daily and professional life, psychology and psychologists have increasingly shaped human interaction.[26] Since the second half of the last century, psychologists have moulded not only the discourse but also the ideal of relations in organisations and management. The same can be said about personal relations such as matrimony, where reflecting on and discussing a couple's relationship has become an important demand. Success in the professional as well the private life depends on self-monitoring. Scanning the relations – being continuously aware of the development of one's relation with others – is not only crucial for communication, but for one's life …at home and at work. This peculiar mix of self-interest and sympathy, of attention to oneself and manipulation of others, articulates a historically new type of selfhood baptised by Illouz as 'reflexive selfhood'. This new ideal of self can be found especially among the members of the new service class, where control of oneself and manipulating emotions is part of the job, e.g. in professions such as those of therapists, consultants and designers. Controlling one's emotions pays! But, as we saw before, that is less so in the case of minorities who are excluded and do not get enough respect.

The last couple of paragraphs are not a defence of a psychological approach to communication. Indeed, in this chapter we have defended the opposite – not to remain in a psychological, individualistic approach when analysing or practicing communication. We cannot isolate others from the groups to which they belong. What matters in the communication process are not only the content, but also the patterns of relations constructed before and outside the immediate situation. People enter a conversation as man or woman, black or white, minority or majority, local or immigrant – identities constructed earlier on in life. If we want to communicate effectively, we should continuously scan positions of and relation with others. Positions and relations are not fixed on a micro level in a meeting, but are to a large extent structured by the context, i.e. the groups one belongs to or is identified with. Conversation is like a dance in which one anticipates and reacts on the movement of the partner, inspired by the music made by others. Who is guiding can change; and sometimes people tread on the others' feet. Continuously, then, we should watch the signals that indicate differences and similarities between the partners. Scanning is essential to situate the interlocutors in social space and to measure distances and positions. As we will see in the next chapters, those positions and spaces can vary from local to global, from the space of daily life to specific cultural fields.

Notes

1. M. Oosterwijk. Internet as personal medium of communication in: *Amsterdams Sociologisch Tijdschrift* Sept.2002 394 – a.f.
2. F. Schulz von Thun (1979) *Hoe bedoelt u? Een psychologische analyse van menselijke communicatie*. Groningen, Wolters-Noordhoff.
3. *De Volkskrant* 24/9/1999

4. Interview VPRO TV 09 04 1989

5. I use here a pioneer study by Trees Pels in *Netherlands Journal of Social Sciences* 39/2 2003, 126-141.

6. Pels o.c. 134

7. Hans Kaldenbach defends in his book *Respect* (2004) that this communication gap is more related to street culture, which can be found not only among immigrant youth but also among local Dutch youngsters.

8. G. van den Brink (2002) *Schets van een beschavingsoffensief*. Amsterdam University Press; Richard Sennet (2003) *Respect; the formation of character in an age of inequality*. New York, W.W. Norton.

9. Stuart Hall (1991) *Het minimale zelf en andere opstellen*. Amsterdam, Sun.

10. See, for an overview, Kath Woodward (2002) *understanding identity*. London, Arnold.

11. P.H. van der Plank (1983) *Taalsociologie* Muiderberg, Cotinho.

12. Eva Illouz (1997) Who will care for the caretaker's daughter? Toward a sociology of happiness in the era of reflexive modernity. In: *Theory, Culture and Society* 14/4 pp. 31-66.

13. Thomas Wartenburg (1990) *The forms of power; from domination to transformation*. Philadelphia, Temple University Press.

14. See: Edward T. Hall (1969) *The hidden dimension*. New York, Anchor books. Albert Scheflin (1974). *How behavior means*. New York, Doubleday.

15. A. Vrij (1991) *Misverstanden tussen politie en allochtonen*. Amsterdam, VU Uitgeverij.

16. P. Bourdieu (1997) *La domination masculine*. Paris, Seuil. Terry Lovel (2000) Thinking feminism with and against Bourdieu in: *Feminist Theory* 1(1) 11-32

17. P.A.Goslin (1993) *How to be a carioca*. Rio, Two Can Press.

18. Willy Jansen (1990) Women who stand like men; body language and social hierarchy in North Africa in: J. and K. Verrips (1990): *Ruimtegebruik en Lichaamstaal*. Amsterdam, het Spinhuis.

19. Defense of thesis by K. Ruys. June 2004. University of Amsterdam

20. A. Giddens (1993) *The constitution of society, outline of a theory of structuration*. Cambridge, Polity Press.

21. Guiomar Giapuscio and Wolfgang Kesselheim. Usted que es? Categorizaciones y contexto institucional. In: Kl. Zimmermann e.o.(eds.) *Lenguaje y comunicacion intercultural en el mundo espanol*.Frankfurt a.M/Madrid, Iberoamericana pp. 104-131.

22. Quoted by Mary Waters (1994) Ethnic and racial identities of second generation black immigrants in New York City in: *International Migration Review* 28/4 p.807

23. Quoted in Miri Song (2003) *Choosing ethnic identity*. Cambridge, Polity press. P 106.

24. Louis Boumans e.a. (2001) *Jongens uit de buurt*. Amsterdam, IISG.

25. Wen Shu Lee (1994) communication about humour as procedural competence in intercultural encounters. In: L.A. Samovar and R.E Porter (1994) *Intercultural communication; a reader*. Elmont, California, Wadsworth Publishing.

26. Eva Illouz o.c.

Chapter 3

THE WORLD OF EVERYDAY CULTURE AND COMMON SENSE

Hair is a political issue! In a fascinating book on culture of the new post-apartheid South Africa, one chapter discusses the significance of different hairstyles by blacks: straightening versus the natural look. Author Zimitri Erasmus describes the preoccupation with hair in the 1970s and 1980s when she grew up.[1] She spent hours at home bent over the basin, washing her hair and straightening it half-yearly – a real operation with 17 complicated steps such as washing, conditioning, straightening, curling and swirling all aimed at straight hair. According to the author's colonial-racist notions of beauty, only straight hair was a good consequence. But, she asks herself, is the natural or 'Afro' look better and more authentic?

Reading this article reminded me of the research I did years ago in a Brazilian slum. One day by chance I was observing two small girls, six and four years old, and I overheard this discussion between them.

'My hair is nicer,' said the oldest one. 'Why,' asked the other.
'Your hair is bad; it is so curled.'

I remember that moment because I realised from then on at what a young age racist ideas can influence their victims. Combing your hair seems to be an innocent, unimportant act, but both the South-African and Brazilian cases illustrate that reality is more complex. Culture, politics and routine everyday acts are linked and influence each other.

In this chapter, using a broad range of literature from very different authors on this topic, I will defend the existence of a space of everyday life, or a 'life world', with a corresponding culture. Everyday culture, with a variation of the definition given in chapter one, can be defined as follows: 'Everyday culture' is the way the members of a household, who occupy a similar position in a social space with specific access to ways of self-reproduction and consumption of (cultural) goods and services, embody this position in their self-evident common sense, practical knowledge and of routine activities, expressing these in a common lifestyle.

Approaches and concepts In order to understand the implications of this definition, we will make a quick *tour de horizon* among the many authors that refer to the idea of everyday culture, often in very different ways. We can find so many names and approaches around this dimension that the German sociologist Norbert Elias concluded that this concept does not deserve the name of 'scientific concept' and that serious scientists should ignore it.[2] We do not take this advice, however. The concept is too relevant to the issue of intercultural communication. It can explain why people feel so committed to certain ideas and values, and why changing them is so difficult.

One of the first sociologists to speak about the world of everyday life was the German exile to the USA, Alfred Schutz, who, inspired by Edmund Husserl, called it 'life-world', or in the original language: 'Lebenswelt'.[3] He puts the accent on the subjective side of the concept – the everyday way of perceiving reality. Schutz postulates the existence of various provinces of meaning, each with their specific way of knowing reality and awareness. The everyday way of knowing is characterised by suspension of doubt, spontaneity, self-evidence and lack of reflexivity. This awareness is different from the awareness of the world of entertainment and play or religion. He explains the specific character of the life-world by reminding us of the culture shock that the 'home-comers' undergo. Home-comers are persons who come back for good to their homes – emigrants who return to their native land, e.g. the veterans returning after some years of fighting abroad. Life at home means having in common with others a section of space and time. People live together and the life of the others forms part of his/her own autobiography, an element of their own personal history. The person, who has left home, is no longer immediately accessible. Of course, it is possible to communicate, says Schutz and, for him, letters are the normal medium.

Today we have a lot of means at our disposal. What remains t. same is that by the mere change of surroundings, other things have become important for both parties; old experiences are re-evaluated, new ones, not accessible for the other, have emerged in each partner's life. And, back to the experience of the returning war veterans, 'When the soldier returns and starts to speak – if he starts to speak at all – he is bewildered to see that his listeners, even the sympathetic ones, do not understand the uniqueness of these individual experiences which have rendered him another man.'[3] The soldier and people who have stayed home, speak different languages. Communication between both is almost impossible. The reason is that they have lived in different worlds and have lived different lives. The home to which the home-comer returns is by no means the home he has left.

This alienating experience can occur also in the case of the expatriate, who returns home after some years of living and working abroad. It is an amazing experience that one's re-adaptation to the home situation – adaptation to the former life and traditions – takes more time and effort than the adaptation needed when first time going to a strange country. Living in primary groups, in face-to-face contact and in the same place, creates a familiar world and familiarity. This familiarity gets lost when staying abroad for several years.

The Suriname-born reporter Brave, who grew up in the Netherlands, decided to return and subsequently wrote a book about the daily struggle to re-adapt again in his fatherland.[5] He describes a scene in which trash collectors do not take his trash away. He runs after them and cries in vain to get their attention. From that moment his trash is not collected: he had said too much. Brave affirms that this abuse of power by lesser officials is common in his country. Each bureaucratic position is a position of power. He tries to explain this behaviour.

In Suriname, general rules do not exist. If a guy does not like you, he will ignore you and your rights. Dutch officials would apply general rules without making any distinction; Surinamese officials act differently. For them, relationships are more definitive. This explanation is in accordance with the common traditional explanation: it reflects the difference between a particularistic and a universalistic society. Does this explanation help Brave to solve his problem? Would the trash collectors

...mselves in this theory? They do not need a theory ...jobs. Ordinary human behaviour cannot be ex-...asily. In Brave's case, he should know that returning ...are perceived as arrogant, and that they should ...place. If not, they are put into place, as in his case.

...analyse a little further the subjective dimension of everyday life with Giddens and Bourdieu. The latter does not use the expression 'daily life practices' very much, but instead often makes reference to common sense. He uses many other names for what he mostly calls 'the world of common sense'.[6] Common sense is defined as 'the meaningful world, a common understanding by all members of a society that makes communication and immediate understanding of others' behaviour possible.' This world of common sense is based on a common habitus or disposition. All agents of a given social universe share certain principles regarding the division and structuring of the social space, the consequence of a common history. These common principles constitute the matrix of all common places: high or low, spiritual or material, light or heavy, unique or common. These common places derive their strength from the fact that they refer back to the most fundamental opposition within the social order, the opposition between the dominant elite and the mass of the dominated, and, as such, can be used wherever fields are organised around similar oppositions.[7] They are based on the dialectics between structures, the common conditions of existence and their interiorisation in the habitus or disposition. In that way the world of everyday culture has two dimensions:

- An institutional dimension, the total of commonplaces used in a society. The common sense functions as a fund of evidence, which assures, within the boundaries of a social universe, primordial consensus about the sense of the world. These natural perceptions and common schemes can be found in all institutions such as family, politics and market, and also in the daily interaction.
- A personal dimension, a common perception of the existing social world, consequence of the interiorisation of existing divisions and differences that makes social world self-evident (often called 'doxa' by the French sociologist).

An illustration of this phenomenon is the self-evidence of male domination, mentioned already in chapter one, evidence that bypasses social groups and classes. The andocentric vision of the world is so evident that it is perceived as *the* vision, a neutral one by men and women. The masculine domination based on biological differences is actually naturalised, as legitimisation of power difference. Social order functions as an overall programme confirming male domination overall and everywhere. Because the small corporal difference between men and women is used as a legitimisation of male domination, everywhere in the world, division of labour and responsibilities – in essence all behaviour – is divided according to gender lines with a natural domination by men. This does not mean that political action against this domination is impossible. '*La domination masculine*' recognises that gay men and lesbians are likely to win the struggles over their sexual legitimacy because of their relatively greater access to cultural capital.

Everyday life is not only about knowledge, as the expression 'common sense' may suggest; it is also about practice. To explain this, Bourdieu puts a lot of emphasis on the difference between practical and theoretical knowledge. In this case, he also avoids the extremes of determinism on the one hand and on the other hand the voluntarism of the rational action model. Human action in everyday life is not a blind execution of rules, but neither a conscious execution of an individual plan or project. It is the habitus or disposition, which constructs the world by a specific, more corporal orientation – like a person who leaps and concentrates him/herself and, in this corporal anticipation, already feels the place of landing. As in learning a sport such as tennis or swimming, the success of the player or swimmer does not depend on the intellectual understanding of the body movement; rather, it is their body that understands and knows. These examples are given with a purpose. Practice is based not on an intellectual understanding of the world, but on an immediate understanding of the familiar world, because the mental schemes put to work are the products of the embodiment of the structures of the world where he/she acts.[8] We have learned to prepare and eat food, for example, according to complicated patterns of taste difficult to explain. Why for instance is gazpacho, a soup, eaten cold?

English sociologist Anthony Giddens has also written about daily life.[9] His approach can complement Bourdieu in this respect. Giddens puts the accent on routines and rituals, which make daily life familiar and viable. He considers routine as what happens normally as the basis of daily social existence. The self-repeating character of daily praxis is the basis of existential assurance and of self-confidence. Giddens refers to existentialist philosophers, like Kierkegaard and Heidegger, focusing on the tragic existence of the human world and the human identity. Trust in others taught in early youth, in the interaction with educators, is essential for self-confidence and belief in oneself. This self-confidence is not given, but has to be developed and protected in daily interactions. We are confident, for example, that the letter we posted will arrive and that the train we sit in will reach its destiny. But we also trust that our colleagues at work will not start a fight when we arrive in the morning. Maintaining daily routine and rituals helps us deal with the fear of the unexpected, which continuously threatens our human existence, especially in this risky society (Beck).

Human identity is not given but must be elaborated like our personal story. It is a real skill to continue the storytelling in continuation with our past while also integrating what happens today. According to Gofmann, as we have seen in chapter two, face-saving mechanisms are essential to identity construction in everyday communication – asking and giving respect for our own and the other's identity, thereby avoiding loss of respect.

Self-reproduction   The authors quoted until now have put emphasis on the subjective side of the everyday culture: awareness, consciousness, and practical knowledge. Neo-Marxist Agnes Heller [10] is more concerned with the objective dimension. She also uses the expression 'everyday life' and defines it as 'the aggregate of individual reproduction factors'.[11] This is an interesting attempt to define everyday life in an objective way. Everyday life is the aggregate of activities belonging to the self, which aim at the maintenance and self-preservation of the own person.[12] For Heller, its essence is the self-reproduction of the human being in contrast to the reproduction of society, realized in common labour.

Heller's book is written in a difficult Marxist jargon and is rather philosophical. Research on housekeeping by the French sociologist, Jean Claude Kaufmann, helps us further.[13] He is able to give nice examples of the everyday practice and its significance. Each morning we start the day with 'the dance of founding gestures' – gestures that have become so much a part of the body that people are not aware of them …raising the hand in a complex movement to put one's hair in order with an object called a comb, or using the cooker to heat water to make tea, cleaning the table of bread crumbs, etc. This dance is a very old one, hiding its importance in its automatism. Its purpose is to define the place of everybody and everything based on cleanliness. 'The gesture which daily recreates civilisation consists of washing oneself and tidying up.'[14] Everyday practice can vary enormously. The daily routine is the result of a development of centuries, but is at the same time always renewed. To be clean is in our everyday routine under the influence of science linked with hygiene, the fear of illness. In other everyday cultures, this idea is linked to religion. For Muslim women taking their weekly bath in the *hamman,* the public bath, it is somehow a religious practice, a condition for prayer. Washing is, for them, more an act of purification than cleaning.

Cleaning dishes is subject to norms, but Kaufman found that even in France it is done in a variety of ways. In a cross-cultural marriage, it can become a source of irritation. An Indian woman married to a German told me how she feels obliged to redo the dishes cleaned by her husband, since he puts all dishes together in the sink and washes them. For her that is not clean. She could not eat from those dishes. For her, the dishes are only clean when rinsed under running water one by one. So she redoes this job in his absence, in order to avoid conflicts.

When we make an inventory of the objective elements of everyday life, we should make a distinction between individual self-care and collective management of the household. Activities of self-care are: sleeping, dressing, eating, washing oneself, urinating and defecating. In the management of a household (independent of its composition, a couple with children or not, male or female-headed household, extended or nuclear family, etc.), we can distinguish the following tasks, and I use official Dutch categories: shopping, childcare, cooking, cleaning dishes and laying the table, taking away dust by sweeping and dusting, scrubbing and polishing, financial, community and health services.[15] Of course, these activities will vary according to the available infrastructure and technology facilitating the household performance. The culture of everyday explains why men and/or women, according to age and social class, perform certain tasks.

Everyday culture worldwide   Practical knowledge can be found in all cultures. In everyday life every human being uses this knowledge. Anthropologist Michael Jackson discovered during research in Sierra Leone how well the women were able to make a cooking fire.[16] His discovery was not made theoretically but by imitating their behaviour, by putting the small wood between the stones under the cauldron and pushing them further into the fire at the measure in which they burned. In the eighties, development consultants were very active in introducing fuel-efficient stoves in developing countries. In designing the stoves, they overlooked the practices of the housewives. The programme proved to be a failure because, in practice, efficiency is not the priority of the cook; speed is what they value. In other places, space heating is another need.[17]

The content of everyday culture can and will vary, and can be very different from our own. For instance, because of this matter-of-fact wisdom, the naturalness of understanding is mixed with extra-natural causes. Clifford Geertz defends the use of the concept of common sense also in the case of Azande witchcraft.[18] In a discussion with the famous Evans Pritchard, he explains that only 'when ordinary expectations fail to hold, when the Zande man-in-the-field is confronted with anomalies or contradictions that the cry of witchcraft goes up. This element does not transcend common sense but reinforces it.' He gives another example: If a man contracts leprosy, it is attributed to witchcraft only if there is no incest in the family, for 'everyone knows' that incest causes leprosy! It is as the Insha Allah for some Muslims or crossing oneself for some Christians, not to enter into religious debates, but to avoid them, and to stick to common sense.

Everyday practice is self-evident – so self-explanatory that we are not aware of it and we accept it without explanation. Only when we enter situations in which people behave differently with the same self-evidence can we discover that what seems evident is only arbitrary. We then understand that our familiar way of doing things is just one of the many possibilities like brushing your teeth (why with toothpaste?) and urinating (why do most men stand when they pee?). The thousands of customs and rituals that make up daily life have been learned with a lot of pain and trouble, so well, in fact, that we have forgotten how much time it took, for example, to learn to write. Can you remember the moment you tied your shoelaces for the first time?

The comparison with the stranger helps understand how a basic framework of perception, a common culture, functions. Common sense makes the agreement in disagreement possible.[19] This means similarities exist together with difference. How do we reconcile this common sense, based on a common habitus on the one hand with the differences in class positions with different lifestyles on the other hand? Again, Bourdieu suggests not choosing between them. Both exist at the same time. A dominant culture does not exclude the existence of subcultures or even counterculture. Common classificatory schemes and different class views and lifestyles are all consequences of a common habitus. The social space knows subspaces. The Brazilian working class is aware that 'in the factory the production comes from their hands, but not from their ideas. Those come from the studies of the engineers.'[20] The division between manual and intellectual labour for working class people is a fact and a justification for differences in position and power. Differences in class positions do not exclude solidarity between them. Solidarity is possible between people placed in different positions: poor and middle class agents. Bourdieu explains this with the similarity of their positions. Both groups suffer under oppression, although of different kinds. This explains why Brazilian artists and writers were capable of writing and performing in subversive telenovelas during military dictatorship, identifying with popular cause.[21]

The divisions in complex societies and the related categories are not only between social classes. Other divisions based on age, gender and sexual orientation play important roles. For the Brazilian workers quoted before, being male is as important for their identity as being workers. Similarities and differences in positions and dispositions can be found in various ways.

Flowing boundaries of everyday life   What is the universe of everyday life? What are its boundaries? Bourdieu is mostly vague about it, however he suggests that common sense is national 'to a substantial part'. Why? Above all, because the educational system has the task of creating the nation as a population sharing the same categories. The main instruments of this symbolic power are, for Bourdieu, the school and the national language. The state determines the school programme and even what is correct writing. The State has a monopoly over the political dimension of society but also influences the common sense directly and indirectly. The State also interferes in the daily life of its citizens by determining categories legally used, like civil state, matrimony, citizen, divorce, etc.

Bourdieu is right about the symbolic violence of the State, however practical objections can be made against his argumentation. Is his view of the school not typical for the French Republican school system – a system that prohibits scarves for the girls up until now, fearing to lose its mono-cultural character ...and refuses to recognise Briton and Corsican as languages? And more in general, is the impact of the school so total? Is it capable of creating common visions and values among all classes? Probably the comic *Asterix* is more effective in creating an image of French history than the school. 'We are all Gaulois', wrote the newspaper *La Liberation*. Compare the research of Paul Willis[22] in the UK and recently Paulle[23] in Amsterdam on the influence of working-class youth, often anti-school and anti-establishment, capable of frustrating the pedagogical efforts to impose a basic common culture.

It is too early to proclaim the end of the nation, but its importance for the formation of habitus is visibly diminishing. Media have become more important for the creation of a common stock of symbols, e.g. youth and sport culture. Watch the opening of the Olympic games. Bourdieu would agree with Beck that the state is a container concept. It is indeed arbitrary, but not empty! As long as this concept is used by people to form their identity, it is real. Also, an imagined community (Anderson) is influencing people's behaviour. Dutch sportsmen who refused to carry the national flag at the opening of the Olympic winter games in 2002 are much commented-on exceptions. Even in the European Union, nation states still have the exclusive right to give passports and to decide who can become citizens and who will be excluded. On the other hand, Bourdieu in his analyses of culture in complex industrial societies, shows how culture, literature, fashion, religion and sport is produced in fields. I conclude that the world of common sense is everyday culture, i.e. culture in so far as specialists do not construct it in specific cultural fields.

The distinction made by Heller seems to offer a better solution for the problem of frontiers between the space of everyday culture and national culture, by focusing on the reproduction of people. However, in reality no clear boundaries can be established between routine activities aimed at self-reproduction and the ones aimed at the survival of the family, respectively the household. Kaufmann found in his research that a wide variety of issues exists in what people must do themselves and what they might possibly delegate to others. The personal and the shameful and intimate seem related. One person will wash her own underwear herself; another will not have others make her bed, as it is too intimate. This suggests that we cannot identify daily life only with household chores, neither with activities aimed at self-reproduction. Everyday world contains a range of activities, difficult to define sharply. It could help us to see culture as a long axe with two poles – at the one hand behaviour in function of reproduction of self and household; at the other end of the axe, we find the public activities practised in cultural fields, which form the opposite pole. How fields are constructed is the theme of the next chapter.

Spaces of everyday culture   How is the everyday culture formed? It is almost sociological common sense to indicate the importance of socialisation in primary groups like the family: children learn how to behave in ways that accord with expectations of the group.

Household   Socialisation occurs in close, face-to-face, personal and emotional relations, mostly in families. For Bourdieu, family is a principle of the construction of social reality.[24] For instance, the transmission of male domination and gender differences takes place mainly within the family. Becoming a man or woman is a crucial dimension of the first socialisation. It is as small children that people incorporate male or female behaviour, i.e. making it part of their body language, and so of the first habitus or disposition. Recently, it became national news in the Netherlands[25] that in a primary school, little boys were stimulated to urinate in a sitting position and not to stand anymore, in order to diminish cleaning costs. A gender difference in a trivial matter of daily life is already a fact when children enter school. It shows again how culture is not so much about values but implies behaviour, learned at home. Rules of courtesy are also learned at home. Those rules have an automatic but profound influence on the seemingly insignificant acts of daily life. But they have a profound meaning: the rules of courtesy reflect the fundamental rules of political order which imposes itself in an unconscious way like the norm – you address your superiors with their title,'Yes, sir or madam!' By learning the different ways to show respect according to the status of persons, youngsters become aware of the different positions persons can occupy in society. In the formation of the everyday culture, the class background of the family is crucial. Bourdieu's *La distinction* gives many examples of how taste can differ according to social class, or more precisely, according to the position the family occupies in the social space.

I will illustrate this social difference with a description of the culture shock a Dutch working-class boy felt, now an adult historian, when he suddenly was invited to an anniversary party of a school friend. He remembers that the boy celebrating his birthday lived in a mansion with a real garden. 'At the end of the afternoon, we were invited to enter the house for dinner. My friend's mother had done her best: fried potatoes, applesauce and meat. Then I panicked. The meat was not cut, as I was accustomed to with my mother. Here you had to do it yourself... I observed for a moment what went on. Then with a throbbing heart I put my knife in the meat. What a disillusion! It was not the easy meat I was accustomed to. Disintegrating under their look. Slowly my elbows rose till above my shoulders in the ineffective struggle with the meat. It did not help when my friend's father, aware of my problem, said: 'Do it as you are accustomed at home.' Never in my life had I felt such a shame. I felt miserably and wanted to puke.'[26] A working-class boy does not learn at home the skills needed in another social environment.

Bourdieu warns us that the concept of family in itself is a part of common sense.[27] It is a 'programmatic' word. And family is not only constructing social reality, but it is in itself a social construction. It gives not only a description but is an element of ordering society. 'That is the basis of the specific ontology of social groups (families, ethnic groups or nations) inscribed at the same time in the objectivity of the social structures and in the subjectivity of the mental structures objectively orchestrated. They present themselves to the experience with the hardness and resistance of things, although they are products of social construction.'[28] Of course under control of the State, private life is public matter for the State, but the control is not total. Gay marriage (in the Netherlands) proves that the concept of family can change under the pressure of social movements.

Processes of socialisation can be found in all kinds of families, but the type of family can also vary enormously. It can vary over time. To give an example, in the Germany of 1800 the family did not matter, but rather *das Haus* (the House), i.e. the nuclear family together with all people depending on the father of the house, who often was an employer too. Other differences exist between ethnic groups, and between the western world and developing countries. So the West-African family is characterised by separate life-worlds of men and women. In the same society we find female-headed households, one-person households, etc.

We cannot underestimate the importance of the family or, broader, the first socialisation in the forming of a person's disposition – the basic cultural pattern of a person. This period in everybody's life is important for appropriating one's own gender role. Learning the mother tongue, the carrier of the basic concepts, is important for the perception of reality. Family socialisation is basic for taste, from food to cultural products, and for learning the basic rules of civil interaction used in face-to-face communication, preferences in sport and all other elements that belong to a certain lifestyle. It seems that the corporal dimension of this first and basic socialisation process is essential. Food, sport, gender and face-to-face communication

are all a direct part of the corporal dimension of human existence. Value systems can change, but the basic daily life culture
is formed during the first socialisation. The previously mentioned German, son of a farmer and raised on a farm without
central heating, has been accustomed to putting on his socks
first of all and taking them off last of all to avoid the cold floor.
As a mature man he remains faithful to this practice learned as a
child.

Kaufman reminds us of the central place of objects in the
production of our existence. In his study on household management he analyses how the objects of daily life help us to form
our own identity. They play the role of assuring ourselves in the
day-to-day activities. Compare the average life of homeless people with that of most citizens. Their possessions and identity
have been reduced to a minimum. A couple becomes a married
couple by sharing things and managing a household together. In
her book *Generations: Grandmothers, Mothers and Daughters* the
Australian Diane Bell shows how significant things passing from
generation to generation carried with them family histories, in
a gendered way. Ways important for women, but overlooked by
men! Things can link bodies across space and time together and
thus embody relationships, although more so for women than
for men.[29] The senses, including smell, play an important role,
as one interviewee told about her grandmother's kitchen.

'I can remember the way Nar's kitchen smelt. Every now
and again I will go somewhere, and the smell is there. Sometimes in the old house down in the Arabana street, in Canberra,
I could smell that in my own kitchen. I always felt good when I
could smell Nar's kitchen in my kitchen... It was not so much
happy as belonging. There is an emotional attachment. Smells
attached as clean, wholesome and nourishing, and the attachment is part of identity: it is warmth, not happiness.'[30] Who is
not confronted from time to time with smells bringing back
strong memories of his or her youth? Smells that remind one of
mom's special recipes?

The existence of everyday culture can be experienced also
in an indirect way by the specific problems that the partners in a
mixed marriage (meaning with a different ethnic or religious
background) have to deal with. Statistical data proving the
problems the partners in mixed marriages have to face are not

available. However, Hondius found in research among mixed couples in the Netherlands that a significantly higher proportion of mixed marriages still end in divorce compared to other marriages.[31] She stresses that acceptance gradually grows as fear of the unknown is reduced. Mixed couples themselves are also often confronted with the unknown – the cultural differences between them. These differences sometimes cause tension, but can also help solve arguments. The partners simply agree to disagree. After all, they *are* culturally different especially at the level of everyday culture.

Interethnic marriages and interclass marriages are exceptions. Partners are sought and found who have similar positions in the social space. What helps the members of a common household to develop a common cultural frame is the house. Bourdieu has given a very exciting example of the way the Kabyle house determines men and women to perform their quite different roles by setting the scene of male and female action and interaction. In most cultural groups, a distinction is made between those parts of the house accessible for guests/outsiders and relatives/insiders. The traditional house in Brazil has an open but covered space in front of the house where strangers are received, not inside the house, which is reserved for relatives. In African households, the kitchen is forbidden for the men. All those scenes and their implicite rules shape not only people's performance but also their identities and dispositions

Neighbourhood   Everyday culture is corporal and material. People live somewhere in a place they belong to. Remember the difference between geographic coordinates and the warm feelings the place of birth or living can evoke. Places are saturated with meaning, issues also of continuous struggle about meaning. People give meaning to places, but the opposite is valid, too. The place can identify a person: she is a real Scott or he is a real Berliner. To say that a person is provincial means more than that he or she is not living in Paris or London.

Due to the identification of anthropology of culture and village, anthropologists today are reluctant to establish a direct link between culture and place. But faithful to the corporal dimension of culture, we have to recognise the link between social and physical spaces. The position in social space correlates with a person's place in the physical space. The link between social and physical space is diffuse and not immediate. It is mediated by the different forms of capital or powers the agents dispose of – by what gives them more or less access to goods and services. This means that the distribution of agents in the physical space and the distribution of goods and services are related, and the social status of the agents determines their possibilities of access. In working-class neighbourhoods of Amsterdam, the life expectancy of people living there is five years lower then elsewhere.

It is no coincidence that, e.g. in Amsterdam, the cultural institutions (art galleries, concert hall) are situated between the Old South and the canal zone – neighbourhoods with high prestige and populated by inhabitants with, on average, more economic and or cultural capital. Social and cultural capital make it possible to put undesired persons at a distance, and to mix more easily with welcomed people and services. The proximity in physical space makes it possible to build relations with important people and to increase the social capital. An elite quarter, like an exclusive club, gives more status to all its inhabitants. On the contrary, life in a poor quarter degrades all the inhabitants. In cities like Los Angeles and Sao Paulo, the rich are able to appropriate public space, e.g. by closing streets for traffic to create safe spaces and exclude outsiders. They consume not only more space but they are convinced that they are entitled to do so. The environment also influences the behaviour of people. Winston Churchill expressed this effect in one phrase: 'We shape the buildings and later the buildings shape us.'

People identify themselves by the places they live in and they are identified by physical space – by their immediate surroundings like neighbourhood or region. Two autobiographical books by sociologists illustrate how the family and the place where you have been brought up can influence not only one's career but professional disposition as well. Richard Sennet wrote a book on *Respect* based on his experiences as a child in a slum of Chicago. Sennet and his mother escaped this environment; he became a well-known professor and author. In this book he shows his ex-neighbours that he did not forget them. On the contrary, living with them has profoundly influenced his work as a sociologist. Pierre Bourdieu recognizes in his *Essay of a Self-analysis* a link between his characteristic way of behaviour like 'a taste for quarrel' and the particularities of his regional origin.[32] In all of his books, Bourdieu often refers to the relation between his outsider position in the intellectual milieu of Paris and his provincial origin.

Not only intellectuals are influenced by locality. Evidence can be found from a lot of different places. In Manuel Castells' specialist view, a common struggle to improve the place is a condition for a cultural identity.[33] For sure it can be a strong factor, but not a necessary one. Research in San Antonio in the USA proved that the local youth identified with their neighbourhood, what framed the way they gave form to their gender identity[34] They mark their local identity even by wearing distinct clothing and using specific slang. At the same time the neighbourhood defines also the structural constraints defining their identity formation. Outside the area those markers are used by employers and/or police to signify incompetence as a worker or criminal status of those inhabitants. Neighbourhood has strong emotional links, too, in the outskirts of Sao Paulo. The space is called *pedaco* (piece) and represents a feeling of belonging which is shared, not only because of the physical space but also by the implied participation in networks of relations combining links between relatives, neighbours, origin and participation in activities like sport and other forms of entertainment.[35] Besides this working class phenomenon, Brazil knows many slums, or *favelas* – spaces of struggle between drug dealers, police and local leaders. To be born and raised in such a space already sets for boys a probable career in crime, in which they have to defend this place with their own blood.

We may conclude now that certainly the nation is not the exclusive space of daily life. Family and nation are social constructions that, as ordering principles, construct society in their turn. They can be perceived as spaces, but it is very difficult to establish the boundaries of their reach. Family, class, neighbourhood, suburb, and regional or ethnic groups are smaller carriers of identity and culture that can overlap each other to a certain extent. They all have, as social constructions, arbitrary boundaries, and they are all bearers of cultural similarities and differences – spaces of subcultures.

Effects of globalisation on everyday culture   In the first chapter, I discussed the importance and influence of globalisation. Once the specific character of everyday culture has been established, it consequently raises the question: what is globalisation's influence on everyday culture? Does everyday life become globalised as some sociologists (Beck, Canclini) suggest, i.e. directly influenced by an expanding common world culture? Of course, the kitchen of most European and Latin American consumers is more global than ever; the media inform everywhere about global news, but most of day-to-day life remains linked to local identities. Academic detachment and a helicopter view on reality do not belong to everyone's lifestyle.

The argument most used to prove the globalisation of everyday life is the crucial role of the media in day-to-day life. Is the far and potentially troubling news invading the near space of the household, a space of ontological security? The concentration of media industry in the hands of a few owners is a fact, however, this does not prove that the broadcasted programmes are the same everywhere. Research on Asian media[36] shows that in Asia the global media adapt to the local situation. CNN, BBC World and CNBC tend to buy local companies in order to produce country-specific programmes. On the consumer side, evidence exists that the consumption of TV products (news and entertainment) is based on active selection in the frame of gender and class. It is mostly in the household that TV is watched, and those circumstances determine the selection and the decoding of the messages. Danish researcher Tufte has studied how this occurs in Brazil. Instead of trying to analyse and compare all the research done on this topic, in the following section I will summarise the findings of this typical and exemplary study.

Tufte did an ethnographic study on poor women watching TV. The women lived in three different neighbourhoods: in a *favela* in Salvador de Bahia, in an old workers' residential area in the far outskirts of Sao Paulo and, finally, in an 18-year-old squatter settlement in the outskirts of Canoas in Rio Grande do Sul. The variety of the places suggests the possibility of differences between the interviewed women. However, those differences seem only gradual. Tufte uses the concept of 'neighbourhood culture' to characterise the common life-world of his interviewees. This concept[37] signifies a new culture, different from the heroic working class earlier last century, or middle class living in the centre of town. This culture emerges as a result of outside influences from e.g. the church and local self-organisation especially by women, who have their own space and networks. Characteristic of this sub-culture is the concern with family, solidarity through social networks, the daily struggle to keep the house decent, class-consciousness and racial discourse as part of their identity. This culture is fragmented and hybrid – a mixture of popular traditions and mass media, of old and new forms of religiosity, with a strong sense of locality.

Before entering into the impact of the telenovelas, Tufte dedicates two chapters to the temporal and spatial dimensions of the novela reception. He introduces another new concept to explain the specific circumstances of the TV reception by the Brazilian proletariat: 'the hybrid sphere of signification', meaning something like the specific way to organise the time of the day, space of the house and social relations in function of the telenovelas. Observing the way the interviewed women watched telenovelas during hours led Tufte to coin this concept. TV in the neighbourhood he researched is watched not privately, but in a group, and at the entrance of the house – a space which is not private or public, but which is organised around the TV set. The stories and characters are commented on and discussed by the viewers. Men and women have their own spaces, but here they interact and negotiate what is watched. Tufte is not explicit about who decides what is watched. While in working-class families in the UK the men still decide[38], women watch the novelas not only at prime time, but also often in combination with household chores. Everyone's routine is influenced by TV in such a way that TV is 'structuring everyday life'[39].

The final conclusions of Tufte's study I can endorse wholeheartedly. They coincide with my own conclusions on the impact of telenovelas on a working-class audience, although the study neglects the influence of the form and proletarian taste for melodrama. Telenovelas contribute to the emancipation of working-class women by offering active role models, far from the Maria stereotype, and helping them in the management of their emotions. Tufte is even more outspoken. He argues that television fiction constitutes a space for different social groups to be recognised and feel recognised, thereby contributing to the articulation of citizen identity among subordinated groups in society. Their own concerns, mainly the suffering as an intrinsic part of daily life, reflected in the suffering of the 'soap' heroines, are recognised as a common concern shared by others. This is the neighbourhood way of exercising cultural citizenship. A really interesting study, it shows again the importance of TV fiction in the lives of millions of poor people in Latin America, and the way in which the media make them participate in public life.

Another question is whether TV entertainment is influencing people's perception of reality. Dorner[40], a German scholar, wrote a book about the development of a new way to realise politics under the influence of USA and TV: 'politainement!' This new expression describes the alliance between politics and the entertainment industry. Politicians look for contact with the audience and potential voters via the media. In their turn, the media like to use politics to increase their audience. The political becomes personalised and, as such, attracts more people. It is interesting to see that Dorner uses Schutz' concepts. Based on the earlier quoted Schutz, Dorner also recognises a specific way to know reality in the field of entertainment, which is realised more than ever on TV. This means that the fictional world is the reality of 'as if'. Different from the daily life world, it makes viewers free from the necessity of real life whereby unknown possibilities for identification are offered. An average person, even a 'looser', can become a hero(ine) or an idol, and bypass daily routine in unimagined ways.

In discussing TV reception, it is crucial to realize the importance of the group background in decoding the TV messages. The perception of the world is not only mediated by TV, but at the same time by their own cultural frame or subculture. I noticed in research on working-class TV reception by Brazilian workers how women could wonder about the autonomy of the middle-class heroines but at the same time realize that this was not for them. So their behaviour became a topic of discussion, but not of imitation. In an article on belongings, Morley uses a similar relativising tone. In his opinion, in spite of Hollywood's impact on global imagination, 'the majority of people have still an effective horizon of action which is very local and often ranges no further than the end of their own street or neighbour-hood.'[41] On the other hand, there is no doubt that new forms of communication, like the Internet, are affecting everyday culture – only we don't know how and to what extent. For instance, Shi-ite women emigrated from Lebanon, although very involved in the Montreal setting, participate at a distance in Lebanese soci-ety via internet on a daily basis.[42]

If we apply the division in basic activities of daily life – self care and reproduction of the household – then we can we see a trend directly related to the model of a consumption society. In self-care, there is an increasing accent on self-presentation. The body has become an integral part of the projects of self-devel-opment …to name some forms: piercing, tattoos, bodybuilding, beauty care and chirurgy, with an exchange and borrowing from other cultures clearly visible in the motifs of tattooing.

In the household, we can observe an increase in the num-ber of objects used, leading to a new profession of household organizers who assist others to get rid of their superfluous belongings. The important role of technology we have already mentioned in reference to TV and Internet, but we cannot for-get about 'new' inventions like the microwave and especially the car. Household activities are changing, but slowly. In a com-parison between 1957 and 1995, most washing is still done on Mondays. As the week progressed, shopping was done more regularly. On Friday most domestic activities were carried out. Sunday lost some of its special character, as more domestic activities on this traditional rest day increased. The division of tasks between men and women is changing. Men participate more in activities like cooking and cleaning, sharing a trend toward a part-time appointment in the household, although from different points of origin. Women still do a lot more in the household. All those changes are related to the fact that more and more women have entered the labour market, albeit mostly part-time.

New means of communication and the shrinking world also can make possible new forms of locality. To give just one example: The Diola is an ethnic group living in the Casamance, the southern region of Senegal. This group has practiced, for time immemorial, initiation rites of the boys in the sacred woods, a condition toward becoming an 'adult'.[43] The secrecy of the ceremonies is an important aspect of their influence: 'It is not the knowledge of the secret that is important, but the prohibition on speaking about it.'[44] In the last decades, many members of the group have emigrated and now live in Europe, mainly in France. However, this did not cause the end of this ceremony. The leaders have them adapted so that the ceremonies are open for participation by the emigrants. It is possible to combine Senegalese or French citizenship and membership of the initiated group at the same time. 'The community's central ritual has been adapted to include global powers…the community has retained the capacity to produce subjects that *embody* translocality.[45]

Characteristics of everyday culture   To summarise our findings, how can we define everyday culture? 'Everyday culture' is the day-to-day, self-evident routine of practices aimed at the reproduction of one's own corporal identity and immediate social environment. It is an embodiment of agents' social position in a social class, gender relations, ethnic group, neighbourhood, region and, often, also nation-state and a consequence of the first socialisation. Everyday culture, as the domain of practical knowledge and common sense, focuses especially on the corporal dimension of human existence, inclusively a person's representation, and is for this reason necessarily more local than other dimensions of culture. This first habitus or disposition is the basis for further personal development and, as the next chapter will explain further, investments in and commitments with (cultural) fields. This is a flexible concept of culture without fixed boundaries. It should be thought of more as a pole of society where the reproduction of the human existence is at stake – a fluid and a more or less autonomous space with the following properties:

- It can be seen as structured around the pole of the routine activities aimed at self-reproduction of one's own person and the household of which one is a part. The boundaries are not clearly defined.
- It is at an institutional level the sum of non-discussed shared visions, evaluations and ways to behave which are self-evi-

dent for people belonging to a certain universe. At a personal level, it has become almost pre-reflexive behaviour.

- It is a consequence of the primary socialisation in the household/family and an embodiment of its social position not only in the Nation-State, but also in smaller social spaces like neighbourhood and region.
- The existing visions and appreciation, consequences of symbolic violence, are self-evident and 'natural' for the members of the same universe.
- Everyday culture offers us practical knowledge, the basis for performing everyday activities, aimed at one's own reproduction and household.
- It is linked to the corporal dimension of human existence; more than to common ideas, to common behaviour, e.g. as man or woman, food and taste, face-to-face and non-verbal communication, and language.
- Because corporal and dependent on objects, it is also more local rather than national or cosmopolitan, depending on social class and related lifestyle.
- Everyday culture has changed always, but is increasingly changing under the influence of technical inventions and globalisation affecting household chores and household organisation.
- Everyday practical knowledge and behaviour at a personal level can be adapted in new situations. This adaptation demands effort and is easier in times of crisis, like a prolonged stay in a non-familiar environment, when the situation is different from the surroundings of which the original disposition is a reflection.

Under the influence of globalisation, everyday culture is changing, but it is not very easy to describe how and in what direction. Studies on the effects of globalisation concentrate on structures more than on the personal and private life-world. The existing evidence permits us to draw the following provisional conclusions:

- The media increasingly structure the daily routine of many individuals and households. Meals, entertainment and sleeping time are organised as a function of media-programmes.

- The time-space compression affects everyday life by the confrontation in one's own home or private situation with events far away. People seem to rely more and more on mediated experience instead of on their direct experiences.
- Not only access to media but also decoding of media content and their acceptation occurs in the framework of existing class and gender relations. This explains also why the effect of the media is far from immediate.
- In spite of time-space compression, humans are as corporal beings always situated in a specific place and time.
- Personal representation can, under the influence of a consumption society, take many forms and, also, people, inclusively men, today dedicate more attention to impression management – their self-presentation – via clothes, hair and makeup.
- Working class and immigrants seem to identify with a place – not with the nation but with a town or neighbourhood. At the same time, the consumption of modern industrial goods, even in small quantities, and especially the consumption of cultural goods – products of a global cultural industry – offers them a way to participate as citizens and to construct their own visible identity and lifestyle.

Consequences for intercultural communication   Recently a new shop opened in Amsterdam catering food for expats under the slogan: 'There is no taste like home!' Everyone who visits Dutch expats abroad knows how you can make them happy with salt liquorice and Gouda cheese. People enjoy typical food from home. In familiar food, people celebrate their original identity. Everyday culture is emotional and not rational, not something that can be explained in a discourse. What for one group is heaven is for others hell. There is no accounting for taste. What is important to realize is the enormous variety in daily life routines.

People can feel as the Germans say *'unheimisch'* – not at home, not at ease, bad – because they find themselves in a strange and unfamiliar country or environment. Even when understanding the language, this feeling is in great part caused by the many small differences between the reality as it appears to be and the system of dispositions and expectations of the everyday culture that a person is trained in. His/her senses are continuously offended (or exited). A western expat living Sana'a, not far from a mosque became so irritated by the early invitation to prayer that he sabotaged the electricity of the installation. Table manners are another sensitive matter. Eating with an open mouth or smacking has in the socialisation process often been loaded with strong negative feelings. I know a case where even love was not able to overcome the irritation of the partner. Cleaning your nose with a handkerchief is for some people disgusting; others dislike blowing the nose with only your fingers. What do you use to wipe clean your bottom? Those who use water find paper disgusting. Other groups use corn-cobs, leaves or pebbles – repulsive ideas for many.

Many ethnographers have made a life of making inventories of cultural differences of people. The variations are enormous in all aspects of human and everyday life, like ways to take a bath: a shower, a sauna, in a tub with soap, or without for the Japanese. There are many ways to organise self-care and household activities. Cultural differences are manifold, but they are not evaluated all in the same way. In the first chapter we have seen that differences can be used as markers of distinction or to stigmatise people. Differences in the sphere of everyday life are emotional and not rational and, for that reason, a purely rational approach is not enough. More than ever a distinction is needed between the person and his or her behaviour, if this causes negative feelings.

Everyday cultural differences can be very obvious and simple to understand. The Dutch-British anthropologist Janet van der Does de Willebois studied the connection between clothing, posture and world view. To do this, she visited three Senegalese villages, an Animist, an Islamic and a Christian village all situated near one another. She observed how Moslims walk with a dignified posture, wearing loose robes. Animists are muscular and care little for clothing, but are proud of their bodies. Christians, under the influence of prudish missionaries, wear tight clothes and walk with bowed heads: for them the spirit is more important than the body. The conclusion: clothing, movement and outlook on life are connected to one another, but also quite different in the same region.[46]

Cultural differences of daily life are not always that simple. This chapter started with the case of hair politics in South

...at illustrated the link between everyday life and ...es like politics. Erasmus describes how the domi-...has changed in post apartheid South Africa, from ...o dreadlocks. Both styles communicate an identi-...king to read how the author is unable to come to ...ons. Hairstyles are a statement, but far from sim-ple. Dreadlocks are not a 'natural style', but an imitation of Afro-Americans ...and whites in South Africa also adopt this style. 'This style has come to present Africanness for both black and white South Africans,' Erasmus concludes. 'There is always a difficulty in the midst of our cultural creations even when the past is present as a transformed past. This difficulty is marked by the constant overt presence of 'race'.[47] Everyday cultural differences are also markers of social distance and inequality. Everyday culture in South Africa has been marked by apartheid, and the struggle against it. For outsiders it is difficult to know, and less easy to feel, what this local tradition means. Communication between people with a different primary socialisation, related to unequal social positions, demands special sensitivity to develop mutual understanding. This is not only the case in South Africa; it applies also to our own societies. I was surprised (that shows I am an outsider) to read in today's paper that last Sunday a congress was organised in Rotterdam about Afro hairstyles.[48] We can look at the importance of everyday culture from another perspective, the dominant Dutch population. How are they performing as emigrants?[49]

How successful are they in adapting to new cultural environments? Take the Dutch immigrants in Australia, for example. They are a special group because one-third of them has returned to the Netherlands. The ones that remained speak English even at home. Most of them have been naturalised. They appear to have adapted, even assimilated. It is true that the Dutch immigrants in Australia tried to behave as ideal immigrants, in spite of low initial identification. Most of them had preferred to go to Canada. The identification remained low because of the hostile reaction of the Australians to the influx of immigrants. How do they see themselves? In their own words, as 'Dutch Australians' or 'foreign Dutchmen'? After so many years they wonder if they have failed as immigrants, because they still feel Dutch. A researcher's evaluation is that their assimilation has been an unrealistic expectation. Similar developments can be found among the Dutch immigrants in Brazil, like in Holambra. This can be explained by the influence of the first socialisation in the immigrant's life. Everyday culture can be adapted; you can learn to speak the local language, but the immigrants in Australia feel after so many years 'yet deep down still Dutch'. We should not expect of ourselves, nor from others living in an unfamiliar environment, to adopt to the local everyday culture. Crucial for effective intercultural communication is to realise that we do not have the right to demand from others that they deny the effects of their first socialisation and adopt or even adapt to our everyday culture. You cannot demand that a person denies his or her personal history.

Adaptation is quite different in the case of cultural fields, the topic of the next chapter. Fields cannot exist without adjustment of all participants. Everyday culture demands a 'familiar' and rather specific environment. Next to localisation, we find globalising trends in culture that facilitate intercultural communication. In the next chapter we will see that there are moments when intercultural communication is not so difficult, because all players in the field are adapted and follow the same rules.

Notes

1. Zimitri Erasmus (2000) Hair politics. In: S. Nuttal and C.A. Michael (eds) Senses of culture; South African culture studies. Oxford, Oxford University Press.
2. Norbert Elias (1995) Sur le concept de vie quotidienne. In: *Cahiers Internationaux de Sociologie* Vol.99 pp 237-246.
3. Alfred Schutz (1964) Collected papers I and II. The Hague, Martinus Nijhoff.
4. Schutz o.c. II p.114.
5. Iwan Brave (1998) *Enkele reis Paramaribo, terug in Suriname*. Amsterdam, Bert Bakker.
6. In just one book, *Meditations Pascaliennes* (1997), we can find the following expressions: 'everyday existence', 'ordinary experience of the familiar world', 'normal existence', 'world of practice', and 'the world of everyday existence'.
7. Pierre Bourdieu (1979): *La Distinction* . Paris, Minuit. p. 468.
8. Bourdieu (1997) *Meditations pascaliennes* p.163.
9. Anthony Giddens The constitution of society. Oxford Polity Press, 1993; chapter 2; Modernity and Self-identity Oxford, Polity Press, 1994. chapter 2.

10. Agnes Heller (1984) *Everyday life*. London etc., Routledge and Kegan Paul.

11. A. Heller o.c. p.3.

12. A. Heller o.c.: p. 27.

13. Jean-Claude Kaufman (1997) *Le Coeur a l'ouvrage; Theorie de l'action menagere*. Paris, Eds. Nathan.

14. O.c. p.21.

15. SCP (1999) *Tijdsbesteding en tijdsordening in Nederland* 1975 – 1997 p.127.

16. Michael Jackson (1983) Knowledge of the body. In: *Man* 18/2 pp.327 – 345.

17. Crew (1997).

18. Clifford Geertz (1983) *Local knowledge* chapter 4, Common sense as a cultural system.

19. Bourdieu (1997) o.c.: p.118.

20. Nico Vink (1988) *The telenovela and emancipation*. Amsterdam Royal tropical Institute.

21. See chapter 5 of my book on *telenovelas*.

22. Paul Willis (1990) *Common culture; symbolic work at play in the everyday cultures of the young*. Buckingham, Open University Press.

23. *NRC* 10/2 /02.

24. Pierre Bourdieu (1994) *Raisons pratiques* p.137.

25. *Volkskrant* 19/2/2003.

26. H. Bellien (2000) *Huis, tuin en keuken*. Antwerpen/ Amsterdam, Uitgeverij Contact. p. 52.

27. Bourdieu (1994) O.c.

28. Bourdieu (1994).: o.c. pp135- 145.

29. John Fiske (1993) *Power plays, power works*. London/ New York, Verso: 208 e.f.

30. Fiske o.c. p.209.

31. But this differential is narrowing. In general, the Dutch have an ambivalent attitude to inter-ethnic couples: curiosity and fascination on the one hand, fear and concern on the other.

32. Bourdieu (2004) *Esquise pour une auto-analyse*. Paris, Raisons d'agir. p.115.

33. Castells (1997) *The power of identity*. Oxford, Blackwell p.60.

34. Harald Bauder, Agency, place and scale: Representations of inner-city youth identities. In: *Tijdschrift voor Econ. and Sociale Geografie* 92/3 pp. 279-290.

35. Jose Guilherme C. Magnani (2002) De perto e de dentro in: *Rev. Brasil. de Ciencias Sociais*, junho 2002.

36. Yu Li Chang (2001). From globalization to localization; the world's leading televisions news broadcasters in Asia in: Asian *Journal of Communication* 11/1 pp 1-24.

37. Borrowed from the Spanish-Colombian media researcher Jesus Martin-Barbero (1993) *Communication, Culture and hegemony*. London, Sage.

38. Liesbeth van Zoonen (1999) *Media, cultuur & burgerschap*. Amsterdam, het Spinhuis.

39. Van Zoonen o.c. p.188.

40. Dorner (2001) *Politainment: Politik in der medialen Erlebnis Gesellschaft*. Frankfurt a.M., Suhrkamp.

41. David Morley (2004) Belongings; place, space and identity in a mediated world. In: *Journal of Cultural Studies* 4/4 429.

42. Josiane Le Gall (2002) Le lien familial au coeur du quotidien transnational: les femmes shi'ites libanaises a Montreal. In: *Anthropologica* XLIV (2002) pp 69-82.

43. Ferdinand de Jong (2001) *Modern Secrets; the power of locality in Casamance*, Senegal. Amsterdam, University of Amsterdam.

44. Kirsten langeveld (2003) *Het geheim van het masker*. Utrecht, University Press p.296.

45. De Jong, o.c.p.138.

46. Van der Does. (2001) Bodywork: dress, demeanour and world view in the south of Senegal doctoral thesis at the Free University in Amsterdam September 2001.

47. Erasmus o.c. p. 392.

48. *De Volkskrant* 2004-06-15.

49. Anneke van Wamel MA Thesis on identity and ethnicity among Dutch immigrants in Melbourne. see : awamel@timboa.nl; T. Ammerlaan PH D Thesis see: ammerlaan.demon.nl.

Chapter 4

CULTURAL FIELDS AS CONTEXT OF INTERCULTURAL COMMUNICATION

Social space is divided in sub-spaces. In the last chapter we analysed the space of everyday life. This chapter will examine another 'spatial' concept: the field – a concept that is crucial for the analysis of the production and consumption of cultural goods in contemporary society and for communication. Bourdieu, the author of the concept, does not offer a clear-cut definition. Fields are relatively autonomous but structurally homologous micro-universes. Every field, whether it is fashion, religion or sports, has its own specific characteristics, because in every field a specific power or capital is at stake. Each field also has specific rules; also the ways of interacting are different. In the world of fashion and theatre, in sport and film, in religion and politics, people have quite different concerns and show different behaviour. What is at stake and the capitals used are in every case very distinct. Each field is the institutionalisation of a specific viewpoint, present objectively in the structure of the field and subjectively in the attitude, the habitus, of the agents active in this field.

Fields in society are distinct, smaller social spaces. When a person wants to participate in that field, he/she should learn the values and practices, the rules and the language of the field. I would like to illustrate this with a personal experience that helped me to become aware of the existence of what I later understood as being fields. During research I conducted in a Brazilian slum in Porto-Alegre, I met the girlfriend of a local drug dealer who was in prison. She asked me to look at a letter she had written to demand the judge to give her permission to visit her lover. It was a letter full of pathos and appealing to the sentiments of the judge. By coincidence, a lawyer was present at that moment in the neighbourhood centre. He looked at the letter and, in five minutes, changed this sentimental demand to visit a loved one into an official and legal request. He changed the letter completely – not only the language and the tone. Sentimental arguments became legal ones. Reading his translation, I could not recognize the original letter, but the new one was probably more effective because it was put in a language that the judge could appreciate. However, what was at stake was not a change of language, but a different perspective, other rules of a different game, a different view on reality. These differences had nothing to do with national cultures but with a specific sub-culture: the field of law.

What is a field?   Bourdieu is not the only one to perceive the importance of systems to explain the division of labour in complex societies. However, not all human activities are organised in fields; that only occurs when people have the same interests. Alfred Schutz, for instance, uses the expression 'provinces of meaning', inspired by the psychologist William James.[1] Those are sub-universes of human experience, like the world of science, the world of religion, the world of madness. However, Schutz's emphasis on subjectivity is different than Bourdieu's view in that what matters in a field are the structural relationships.

Structures   The structure of the field is dependent on positions – positions of power – determined by the resources linked to them. What matters in the ongoing struggle are not the conscious strategies elaborated by the parties involved, but the constraints and chances of their positions and the images the agents have of their positions. Fields are specific but also have common characteristics that determine their objective structure. They have in common relations between positions of power and struggles for interests. The structures of fields are very similar because they are determined next to the tension between positions of power and the subordinated positions, by the opposition between the established and the newcomers. In the fields, a permanent struggle is going on. On the one hand are those actors who monopolise the specific authority or capital in the field. They are inclined to use strategies of conservation because they can only lose by change. They are the defenders of orthodoxy and traditions. On the other hand are those participants with less capital – newcomers, mostly younger people – who tend to use strategies of subversion, heresy or originality. What is at stake in the fields is to occupy or maintain positions and their related power to impose visions of what is the law, what is the truth, what is fashion, what is art, or what is politically correct, etc. The structure of a field is determined not so much by outside influences but, first an foremost, by the power relations inside the field – by the struggle between the agents for the monopoly in the field (this can be over taste, faith, competence or knowledge) and others trying to overtake this position.

The subjective side   The fields have more or less the same structure, but each is also specific. They concentrate on a specific good but also demand a specific attitude of all people who are involved. Each field is the institutionalisation of a specific point of view on reality that expresses itself in a specific disposition. These particular views on reality have the pretension to be universal, e.g. artists tend to see the world with a painter's eye and scientists look at reality from a scientific point of view. The fields demand of their players a specific attitude, belief and commitment. You cannot participate in the field without accepting the rules. Becoming a priest entering the ecclesiastical field without belief, for example, is impossible. What we have seen before about the first, general disposition related to practical knowledge and common sense is applicable also in the case of secondary disposition, or rather the original disposition, adapted to a field. 'As the product of the incorporation of a principle of vision and division of a social order or a field, the habitus creates a practice adjusted to this order or field.'[2] Training and/or a long practice will adjust a person to an appropriate attitude – its appropriateness visible in details of body language – and to a field. Examples are clerical behaviour or artistic flair. Disposition is an active principle. As a system of attitudes 'to be' and 'to do', it is a desire to be that seeks to create the conditions of its realisation. Each field supposes its own disposition. To become a participant, not only as a producer but also as a consumer, demands training, often for long years, or at least an investment in time. A specific disposition is the condition for entering a field, or better yet, a similar and flexible disposition open for restructuring and re-socialisation. Initiation, training, schooling and study assure the adaptation that can take years. This can happen informally, like Mozart playing as a child, or in specific training institutes like seminaries for the clergy. Finally, in Bourdieu's opinion, personal happiness depends on the measure of the functioning of the world or a field that makes it possible to develop and realize the habitus of people participating in them.[3]

All these characteristics, the objective and subjective, explain why a cultural field functions like a subculture. Look, for instance, at the field of plastic art, a field with its own rules traditionally expressed in the slogan: L'art pour l'art. A traditional taboo in this field prohibits its artists from putting interest in money first. What matters is aesthetics; the struggle going on in this field is about 'what is art?' This question is topic to passionate discussions, except the artists in this field have the last word. Early in the 20th century, Marcel Duchamp sent a urinal to an exposition, and it was accepted and exhibited. For most outsiders this is impossible to understand. How can such an object be perceived as art? Art is clearly what is defined as such by artists. It's not the objects in themselves that matter but the way the expert – the insider – looks at them. Art is defined in the field of art itself and not outside of it.

Scientific versus practical knowledge   In the last chapter we saw the importance and specificity of practical knowledge as part of everyday culture. In public opinion this knowledge has no status compared with theoretical or scientific knowledge, in spite of the fact that the world in which people think is not the world in which they live, according to French philosopher Bachelard. Theoretical knowledge is not the product of an individual genius in isolation or in a lab. Science is produced like all symbolic goods, in a field. The condition for the production of science is to be free from the burdens and limitations of everyday existence. Scholars are traditionally free from economic necessity and the exigencies of the human body, although at universities today they complain about their administrative burden.

In his writings, Bourdieu has strongly criticised scientists – social scientists included – because they often use their own models, based on scientific knowledge in order to explain daily practices of others. Let me illustrate his critique with an example of an anthropologist in action. Anthropologists are specialised in understanding human behaviour in other cultures. The British anthropologist Nigel Barley did research among the Dowayo's in North Cameroon, resulting in a scientific study and some very funny reports, which made him well known.[4] Barley tells how difficult it was for him to understand this ethnic group and to construct a logical and comprehensive world vision: 'The need to sift...through three tons of rubbish for each ounce of gold extracted' to find relevant information. An example in his own words illustrates how this gold digging was done.

'Why would you do this?' I would ask.
'Because it is good.'
'Why is it good?'
'Because the ancestors told us to.'
(slyly) 'Why did the ancestors tell you to?'
'Because it is good.'[5]

Interviewing did not bring deeper insight, but with the use of structuralist theories Barley is able to create order in the 'chaos' in which this society seems to be, by making a symbolic relation between the domains of food, sexuality and physical space (e.g. the cauldron, the vagina and the jungle!). Barley tries to make a map of the Dowa's' culture by relating rituals to ordinary objects. Could the Dowayos themselves read these maps as something concerning them? The anthropologist is always posing impossible questions, like a child asking the reason for the curved shape of bananas. Most adults do not answer this kind of questions. This knowledge is self-evident and does not need reflection or theories. How can you, asks Barley again, know if the zipto (an herb used as medicine) is useful against headache or adultery? The given answer is: 'By trial and error; what other way?'[6]

Barley suggests, then, that there is a difference in culture at stake: logical thinking versus pre-logical. His interpretation illustrates, besides ethnocentrism, the difference between theoretical and practical knowledge. Bourdieu would see this as an example of an ethnologist who puts his own theories into the heads of others. Scientists pretend to be able to know what people are thinking when acting. They project their models, which suppose an interest in theories that people mostly ignore. Practice has its own logic, which is not easily accessible for science. The ethnographer also remains an outsider who often stimulates the interviewees to look at their practice with a theoretical view. In everyday life, however, scientists also do not understand their own practice. The marriage of the psychiatrist will not last, for instance, if she treats her husband as a patient. For the physicist, the sun also 'rises and sets', although astronomy teaches differently. And even a medical doctor, abandoned by medical science, is capable of consulting magical practices to find a cure.

In spite of this critique, sociology and anthropology have, in Bourdieu's view, a specific vocation. They should create liberty and options by identifying and analysing the structural constraints for agency and showing alternatives.

Who is involved? Lahire[7] reproaches Bourdieu that his field concept is elitist because only the experts and professionals are participating in the fields. But what, he asks, is the role of others like maintenance personnel, cleaners, secretaries and administrators active in fields like sports, religion or science, and the life of scientists, sportsmen and women or religious professionals outside their fields? Don't they have a life outside the world of sport and religion, for example? Lahire is right in asking those questions, but he ignores the dimension of everyday culture. He is equally wrong when he assumes that the social space is identical to the sum of all fields. We have seen that this is not the case. Everyday culture is not a field in its own right; there is no common interest or struggle for a specific capital, however it is an important pole of culture in its own right.

Lahire is right in his critique that Bourdieu shows more interest in the production of cultural goods than in the distribution and consumption of these products. Indeed, people may participate in fields as producers – as historians of the field even as amateurs, consumers and maintenance persons. But all those positions are not the same, as in the field of film directors such as Fellini, and the main actors have more power than stand-ins, and certainly more than the cinemagoers. Although also as consumers, people sometimes need specific 'cultural capital' to be able to enjoy classical music or plastic art. Bourdieu has analysed this in *La Distinction*. During his research Bourdieu found a clear correlation between the consumption of cultural goods and level of education. Taste for cultural products like music is capable of placing people in social space. Further analysis led to the conclusion that three clear distinguished groups could be discerned. The legitimate taste of those factions of the dominant class that are rich in cultural capital entails the ability to recognise legitimate works as worthy of admiration in themselves. This taste presupposes an aesthetic disposition, i.e. the perception and appreciation of cultural goods in terms of form rather than function. The middlebrow taste is the middle-class preference for the minor, more popular works within the major arts. And lastly, the popular taste, which refuses to accept any aspect of all that is formal game and wants for all participation in the spectacle through feelings and identification with the characters.

To these differences in taste correspond different kinds of cultural production. At the one end we find high in legitimacy the pole of restricted production. At the other end with low prestige there is the pole of large production: 'music for the millions!' What are the differences between them? Restricted production is aimed at a small group of insiders, the avant-garde, mostly the cultural producers themselves. The pole of large production has, according to Bourdieu, no legitimacy. Their practice is by definition 'vulgar' because they are directed to as large an audience as possible. Their producers are primarily interested in economic profit. For the consumption of their products, no special knowledge or cultural capital is needed. The products are adapted to the average taste of a general public. Between those two poles all kinds of intermediary products can be found. Going from top to bottom in the hierarchy of taste: the pure avant-garde, the avant-garde becoming accepted and established, the works of legitimate bourgeois art, the works of medium art, the works of vulgarisation intended for the mobile fraction of the middle class, and finally the mass culture products without any distinction. It is important to heed Bourdieu's warning to avoid finalist biases. The intentions of the various producers do not determine their audience. On the contrary, it is the position of the artist in the fields that determines the status of his or her product and audience. The relation between product and the position of the actor in the field is at the same time the key to understanding the work. Marxism saw cultural production as a superstructure that could be explained by the changes in the economy, the infrastructure of society. Other schools like semiology will explain a cultural product such as a novel or painting by its intrinsic structure. Others again try to understand a work by the biography of its maker. The theory of the field will analyse the link between position, disposition and production inside the field. The position in the field is analytically the most important because it refers to the objective side of the field.

Autonomy and borders   Talking about being inside the field prompts the question: What are the borders of a field; what is inside and outside? This is not easy to answer. The autonomy of a field is not absolute. Further, it depends on the efforts of the people participating in the game whether the field will become more or less autonomous or just a sub-field. The boundaries are, in Bourdieu's descriptions, always fluid – not only between different fields, but also in bigger fields and sub-fields, e.g. between sport and football, or science and social sciences.

The concept of field is constructed to answer a traditional question in sociology already discussed by Durkheim and Weber as the social division of labour. Durkheim already demonstrated that from a certain volume and a certain density, society enters into an automatic process of the differentiation of functions. This process often takes the form of professional specialisation that ends in autonomy of those activities in relation to others. Norbert Elias[8] has illustrated this process in the field of music by showing the dramatic position of Mozart who, as an artist, was not able to escape from the obligations and limitations of his position as a courtier. Some decades later Beethoven was, thanks to his aristocratic friends, an independent musician. This process of continuous further specialisation continues and also creates new cultural fields, such as photography first being seen as part of the art of painting, and film originally seen in the sphere of circus and vaudeville. According to Bourdieu, a clear sign of autonomy of a field is the presence of conservators dedicated to the preservation of the life and works of the founding fathers of a field. So the history of the field should be studied.

In practice, if we communicate in fields or in between them, we do so mostly as members of organisations or institutions. Therefore, before entering the practice, let's look at some characteristics of organisations in order to situate them in the approach used in this book.

Organisations and institutions   Global society is becoming 'an integrated web of overlapping organisations.'[9] This process drives the integration of the lives of ordinary people into a number of organisational affiliations, each with different tasks and different forms of control and gate keeping. Via organisations, all human action is increasingly transformed into social processes. This increases control on individuals, but at the same time opens up new opportunities. The specialist Ahrne distinguishes four basic categories of organisations: family, state, private enterprises, and voluntary associations. It makes sense to add a fifth category: international organisations. In spite of all differences in size, objectives and social cohesion, organisations have common characteristics. Four features characterise organisational interaction:

Affiliation: Indicated by uniform, label, location or passport. There are clear distinctions between members of organisations and outsiders. For example, you belong to a firm by employment, to a family by birth or marriage.

Collective resources: All the resources of the organisation can help its members to cope with the uncertainties of the environment. But not all members have the same access to the resources, which also can vary enormously between the organisations. Compare, for example, the gross national product of the United States with that of Mozambique.

Substitutability of members: An organisation is more than the sum of its affiliates. Each individual member can be substituted, and even a state overcomes the substitution of its head or president.

… members gain by access to resources and
… to their affiliation, they lose in autonomy and
… Marriage brings each spouse more responsibili-
… ntrol a state exercises over its citizens can be com-
… power an enterprise holds over its employees.

I… …ion to those four elements, organisations have in common that of being *mental frames*, collective ordering principles
that construct and guide the members' behaviour. No organisation would exist without individuals. Still, the structuring of
human interaction within organisations is independent of any
particular person. Rituals and other forms of socialisation make
for the employees a form of interaction, which is taken for
granted. This institutional principle applies also to the other
forms of organisation.

The terms 'institution' and organisation' are often used synony-
mously in everyday language. In sociological English, however,
they mean different things. *Institutions* are the rules of the game,
which guide and constrain individual and group behaviour;
examples are kinship, private property or marriage. In a few
cases, where they are particularly deep-rooted, organisations
are identified as institutions, e.g. the Church of Rome and the
Bank of England. Institutions can be defined as a framework of
rules for achieving certain social or economic goals. *Organisations* differ from institutions in that they refer to the team playing the game and not so much to the rules of the game. Organisations could be described as the coordination of activities by a
group of individuals with the aim of achieving some common
goal. Organisations thus refer to the specific structural forms
that institutions can take. Bourdieu's concept field is similar to
the concept institution. Field can not exist without concrete
organizational forms: sport as a field needs teams and competi-
tions. Film needs producing companies and cinemas. The field
of literature can not exist without reviews, publishing companies and libraries. In the same way that all newspapers, week-
lies and, of course, TV news groups form the journalistic field.
    In the last decades especially, organisational culture has
become a new subfield of management studies. Organisational
culture can be defined as the cluster of norms about how the

work should be done in an organisation and how people in an organisation should cooperate. Developed as a management tool by consultants more interested in gaining a living more than in academic truth, this kind of study is applied to interventions like organisational change and staff motivation. The models developed by these consultants are very similar.[10] Comparing them proves that those models are based on similar dimensions like formality versus informality, and hierarchy versus democracy. In my view, they give more of a history of organisational development, from the power-oriented private enterprise to the bureaucracy based on the functions – via task organisation in which task performance is the criterion used – to the actual constellation in which personal relations are the constructive principle.

A workaholic is the name we give to somebody working in an organization that is identifying her/himself totally with the organisation. These workers are the exception. More often than not there is a gap between individual interests and the interest of the organisation. Never will attention to organisational culture be able to bridge this gap. This means that, in practice, the organisational culture will be a merger of the norms and values of the field it is active in, e.g. the medical profession, and at the same time of the local everyday culture of the individuals active in this specific organisation ... how doctors and nurses behave at home, for example.

To finish this section on borders of the fields: are they allways national? In most of the fields that Bourdieu has studied at large, like literature, photography and universities, he focuses on the French society. However, he recognises explicitly that economy and sciences are turning into trans-national fields.[11] They are trans-passing national borders. Before analysing what this trans-nationalization of fields implies, we give some attention to recent trends in the fields of cultural production, which preoccupied Bourdieu very much and which he warned against frequently.

Commercialisation?   Another important aspect of the cultural fields is their hierarchy. The existing hierarchy is based on the relation to the field of power. That is the field where it is decided what the forms of capital are – economic or cultural –

and which are recognised as most relevant or important. It is clear for Bourdieu that the economic field in the strict sense occupies a top position, so dominant, in fact, that its preoccupation with profit and calculation has become the model for many fields.[12]

Traditionally, the commitment in cultural fields like arts and science has been very distinct from profit making, a commitment typical of the economic field. Bourdieu sees this independence in relation to commercial interests under siege. The commercial logic penetrates into all phases of the production and circulation of cultural goods. The neo-liberal gospel of the market is preached also for the cultural producers as a solution for all their problems. Defenders of the market as a guiding principle also in the cultural sector use the argument of its democratic character. It is the choice made by the consumers that will decide what will be produced and circulated. Bourdieu is aware of the fact that his reproach will be labelled anti-democratic, with the accusation of elitism and snobbism the obvious reaction. It *is* true that he sounds somehow apocalyptic about content of mass media, but he makes a point. Almost a decade earlier he had started polemics about journalism, wanting to demonstrate that via the audience ratings of TV, information had become commercialised. In spite of the strong reaction of the journalists against it, Bourdieu's analysis[13] is not directed against this professional group. He is concerned with the influence of TV on the cultural fields. As with other cultural fields, journalism is structured by the opposition between serious press and commercial press; between the media working for profit and attracting big audiences via, for example, info-entertainment. On the other hand, the press is focused on their own rules of the field, i.e. the professional ethics of being neutral – a kind of lockkeeper, an intermediary between public and opinion leaders. This pole of the field is interested in maintaining its autonomy in relation to the field of power. The other is, because of the enormous investments needed, more and more depending on an industrial capital. According to Bourdieu, because of the influence of commercial TV, reaching a big audience has become more important for all the sectors, even the more 'serious' press. This has important consequences for the selection of the themes dealt with, the way to present the information, and the selection of the sources of information.

Dominique Marcetti did a comparative study about the foreign news slot of TV news in the USA and Western Europe, more precisely about the so-called international images diffused during the news.[14] She found that general public access to international images is falling because the channels reaching big audiences have cut the time devoted to foreign news, shown now on trans-national channels aimed at more restricted audiences. Secondly, international images are produced by an ever-smaller number of mainly private audiovisual agencies. Finally, economic logic get a bigger grip on this market; international news is increasingly produced at the least cost.

In spite of this evidence, Bourdieu is too negative about TV journalism and the media. It is not true that journalists are only their masters' voice. On the production side we can find what Bourdieu calls homology, i.e. identification by the producers (writers and others) with the subaltern classes and their interests in their society. I found evidence of this identification and preoccupation from the side of telenovela writers and stars in Brazilian commercial TV during military dictatorship.[15] Journalists can play an important and independent role in development and defence of human rights, like increasingly independent groups do via Internet.

Next to Bourdieu's pessimist view on changes in the media field, I would like to mention Manuel Castells' idea of a network society and the possibilities this offers to alternative movements.[16] This is a society where the key social structures and activities are organized around electronically processed information networks. So it's not just about networks or social networks. It's about social networks which process and manage information and are using micro-electronic based technologies. In Castells' opinion this development can go both ways. You can use the Internet to exclude, because you can exclude in terms of access to the network – the digital divide. On the other hand, the Internet is an extraordinary instrument for creation, free communication, etc. One of the greatest surprises for Castells has been that suddenly all these movements that were supposed to be traditional, unable to understand modern processes, are organizing themselves on the Internet, and using information technology and information systems to actually introduce counter-trends to a one-dimensional logic of pure money and instrumentality. Take, for instance, the environmental movement. What most environmentalists do, with the support of scientific experts, is assess through the multiple interactions of systematic thinking what we are doing with our planet, with our environment, by measuring or trying to measure and trying to extrapolate the consequences of certain types of modes of production. The uses of the Internet are allowing the environmental movement to be, at the same time, local and global – local in the sense that people are rooted in their problems, in their communities, in their groups, and in their identities ... but then they act globally. So it's not, as activists used to say, 'think globally, act locally.' No, no: think locally – link to your interest environment and act globally, because if you don't act globally in a system in which the powers are global, you make no difference in the power system. Castells gives us a good example of a general trend: fields or networks of institutions and people are bypassing national boundaries.

Fields become trans-cultural   The network society makes increasingly economic political and cultural institutions transnational; they bypass the national borders. The same is happening in the cultural fields, they become transcultural, bypassing national borders and cultures. Globalisation does not lead to homogenisation of cultures in the world but, yes, to exchange and hybridisation.

Cultural fields, as systems of symbolic production, distribution and consumption of a specific cultural product, mix local traditions with global rules of the game on all levels, determined by the power relations between the agents active in this field on an international scale. Fields bypass more and more national boundaries; examples are sport, film, popular music, but also art, science, health and religion. Let us first elaborate on the field of popular music. Again, I will use studies by specialists in those fields.

Rock music   This genre knows many forms, in constant change; it is a mix of local styles with international musical idioms, which originated in the Anglo-Saxon world. One of the first to describe this exchange between local and global music styles has been Motti Regev.[17] In spite of the rapid changes in this field, he offers a interesting model to explain the global exchange of musical genres. He explains how for an increasing number of musicians and fans in a lot of countries, rock music is an important way to emphasise local identity. In many places in the world, local varieties of this international rock-idiom can be found. Chinese 'xibei-feng', Algerian 'pop-rai', Israeli 'mizrakhit', Argentine 'rock nacional' and Zimbabwean 'jit' are only a few examples. Japanese rock and Fiji rock are forms without their own name. Internationally, rock knows many varieties, sub-fields and positions. Rock is used here in the broadest sense of the word, being the dominating style of popular music since rock-'n-roll in the fifties – a complete break of style in popular music. Since that moment, rock has renewed itself over and over again. New styles and kinds have been developed, partly as reactions to the commercialisation of earlier types. In more than forty years of rock, an enormous stock of knowledge has been developed: artistic styles have been analysed, periods have been studied, and the taste for the production and consumption of this kind of music has been developed. Metal, hip-hop and rap are all varieties of the same international musical language. Musicians all over the world have developed a special skill to make this kind of music, and this special way to make music will be identified everywhere in the world as rock. This global musical language mixes, according to Regev, with other musical traditions, local or national. This mixture can be produced in different ways and results in original kinds of music. What is meant here are not the complex mixtures, which are typical for Anglo-American rock music. What are at stake here are mixtures between this musical idiom and local musical traditions outside this region of the world. The way in which musicians from Aster Aweke to Papa Wemba produce rock music and the audience enjoys it is certainly not homogenous, but its meaning is the same. 'Rock is often used to distinguish a new, modern, contemporary, young, often critical and oppositional form of local identity of older and traditional forms of this identity.' The international idiom is used to fortify its own identity. Chinese rock musician Cui Jian expresses this mixture of global elements well: 'Rock is worldwide. During the festival of Roskilde in Denmark I was the only Chinese, but I felt like at home. Yet there is a difference. I think in Chinese, I feel Chinese, I use Chinese images.'

Back to Regev's analysis. How are local musical traditions integrated into the global field of pop-music? Regev distinguishes three basic forms. First is the pure adoption of Anglo-American rock as a symbol of the modernisation of the local culture. During the 'cold war', rock has been used by East European youth to create their own space and oppose the regime. Secondly is the imitation, which may vary from producing at a local level of Anglo-American rock (as in the case of the Dutch group Shocking Blue that in 1970 internationally made a hit with 'Venus') to the creation of their own local variety, often in their own language as a protest against the establishment, as occurred in Argentina during the military dictatorship. Finally are the hybrid forms in which rock elements are adapted in a selective way and mixed with traditional local style. Examples are the rai-music from North Africa, a mix between French and North-African cultural elements, and the bhanga-rock of the Asiatic community in the UK, used to create a new ethnic identity.

The third form is the most interesting because it implies influence of the local music on the global field. The questions are how and how much? Regev does not answer those questions. Research on the structure of the international music industry by Malm and Wallis showed the complexity of this field.[18] Both Swedish researchers pointed out the growing concentration of big record companies. During the last decade, this trend has become even stronger. Only five companies dominate the field: Sony (revenues $ 6.7 billion), Universal (6.2), BMG (4.7), Warner (4) and EMI (3.5).[19] Since the Dutch corporation Philips has sold Polygram, this sector is still more dominated by Anglo-Saxon companies. This concentration certainly does not facilitate the creation of new local forms of music. The giants in the industry do not like to take risks and prefer that small independent recording companies develop new talent. Those companies, if successful, are often absorbed by the big ones, as in the case of Virgin, once independent and bought by EMI for a billion dollars.[20] In spite of this trend to concentrate, new forms develop, like rap in Africa. This is certainly the case in Latin America, especially in Brazil. Already at the end of the sixties, Caetano

Veloso and Gilberto Gil together developed 'tropicalism', a new form of Brazilian popular music influenced by international pop music. Their inspiration has been Joao Gilberto, the father of Bossa Nova, an earlier mix of Brazilian music and international idiom. In tropicalism, Gil and Veloso integrated the rock of Bill Haley and Chubby Checker, but above all the music of the Beatles. Since then this process of exchange and hybridisation has only intensified.

The global film system   Some years ago Bart Hofstede published research on the international position of the Dutch movie.[21] His conclusion is surprising: contrary to much pessimistic information, the position of Dutch film is not that bad. Although Hollywood dominates this world, the Dutch film industry has carved out its own space in the global world of the movie. Point of departure for this study is the existence of a trans-national system of movie production and distribution, concentrated around the Hollywood industry, but also by a mutual dependency between film world's centre and periphery. The system is truly global. 'This means that nowhere in the world national or regional systems of movies are free of the international influence of the global system, even in a small way.'[22]

Hofstede describes the system as a network of elites, in which alliances and struggle alternate. Film producers, sponsors and organisers of movie festivals depend on each other. The relative position of a national film-field inside this system is dependent on four factors: the language of the movie (languages like Portuguese and Dutch are a handicap), the size of the local production and market, strategic alliances with authorities (subventions or not), and the capacity of directors to innovate. In this system, three sub-systems can be distinguished ...first, Hollywood as centre of the system. Hollywood produces films according to market principles — films that satisfy their audience. Secondly come the independent movies that will not be commercial. These movies show an original vision and a clear intervention by a writer. What both kinds of movies have in common is that they are distributed on a worldwide scale. This is different in the case of the third sub-system of national cinema, which is often distributed via TV and with the support of the government. It contains all genres and is produced in the country-specific language. Those films are primarily local-oriented, strongly decreasing the chance of being sold on the international market, often because they aim at the fortification of national identity.

How do we explain the Hollywood dominance? Hofstede gives four arguments. First of all, Hollywood uses a big home market. This does not imply that Hollywood is the only important movie industry. The Indian film industry is actually bigger, producing more movies (800 to 1000 each year). The distribution of Indian movies, especially in Africa, is very important. But besides the USA home market, Hollywood embodies other advantages: support for export by its own government, the English language used in the movies, and the capacity to innovate.

Distinctions between the sub-systems carry no clear boundaries. Hofstede emphasises the flowing boundaries between the three sub-systems and the mutual dependency and influence. Movies from the periphery of the system were influenced strongly by Hollywood during the sixties. Young directors from Brazil also had a real impact. Further, Hollywood's industry got a new élan during the seventies by buying many of those competitors. In spite of Hollywood's domination, a global system of movie production and of mutual influence between the global level and the local traditions has been established. However, Canclini rightly points at fundamental change in this field[23]. He found in research on media use in Mexico that many film houses have been closed. In less than a decade the video has, next to TV, become the principal form of film watching. Although film does not play the central role, as it once did, in the formation of popular identity, people throughout Mexico today have access to video clubs and/or TV, and not only in big towns. North American films are dominant and are even seen as 'the film'. Film has become part of the audio-visual field of video, and of its international production and distribution. New media like PCs, with their analogue technology, will increase this trend of convergence of media markets. At the same time in English-speaking Africa, video film has become a local alternative. Hundreds of locally produced video films challenge Hollywood's monopoly. In Ghana for instance, around 24 companies are active in pro

ducing video films that are very much in tune with local problems and aspirations. [24]

Gay subculture   A trans-cultural field of quite a different
nature is the gay subculture, often half-clandestine, and sometimes still underground, but present in most countries of the
world. The famous Spartacus guide, a travel guide for homosexuals, written with the cooperation of the target group, demonstrates this global character. In the last years, several sociological studies have been published about the gay existence in Latin
America. [25] For the following analysis, I will use own observations and those studies.

Richard Parker did anthropological research about the gay
scene in Brazil, in which he places this local subculture explicitly in a global context, making his research very relevant to this
book. The point of departure of his study is the gaze, which is
necessary to map the social space of this subculture – a subculture often based on a glance, on merely looking at each other in
a certain way. As one of Parker's interviewees explains: 'You can
pick up people anywhere – on the street, at the beach, in the
shopping centre. You have to give them just that look (dar aque-
la olhada) and they know what you want.' [26]

The gay subculture in Brazil has been strongly influenced
by the traditional gender role of the supposed active men and
passive women, roles transposed to the gay scene. [27] Since the
seventies, this pattern changed drastically once homosexual
relations in the big cities of Rio de Janeiro and Sao Paulo started
to follow the Anglo-European pattern, with many more role models: Barbie (bodybuilders), boys (young queers), gay-activists,
Aids-helpers, etc. Parker offers several explanations for these
changes: the processes of industrialisation and urbanisation,
migration and tourism ...not to mention the emergence of a
commercial gay subculture with bars, dance halls and shops.

This gay subculture is marked in Brazil by an essential characteristic of Brazilian society: the strong and distinct class differences. As phrased by one of Parker's interviewees: 'At some
level, of course, homosexual desire cuts across these kinds of
distinctions, creating possibilities for interaction. Sexual relations that cut across class lines are common. Class differences
can even become part of the erotic game, but class differences

are never forgotten in these relations – class is always present, and you can never escape from it, even when you don't acknowledge it openly or talk about it. It is not like in the United States, where gay identity, or even identification as gay or lesbian, seems to be more important than everything else.'[28]

Parker agrees but, in his opinion, in today's Brazil aiming at modernisation, to assume a gay identity can be part of social ascension. To be a homosexual is identified with the United States or the lifestyle of the elite and middle class, an aspect of the consumption culture. Even youngsters from a favela can participate in a modern lifestyle in this way by their clothes and pattern of spending their free time. The gay economy has done more for the emancipation of the Brazilian homosexuals than the organisations of gay activists, struggling for their emancipation. New identities coincide with global patterns of consumption, part of the globalisation process. Another element of this process is the tourist industry: foreigners visit Brazil, but also many Brazilian gays go to the USA or Western and Southern Europe. People from other Latin American countries immigrate to Brazil, while a lot of Brazilian sex-workers emigrate from their country. Many travel for a freer and better life, but also because of health reasons – to find remedies against Aids.

Interesting are Parker's findings about tourism in Brazil, what can easily be called sex-tourism. It's interesting because he gives a more positive image to the interaction between tourist and local gays than most writers do (e.g. Hodge writes about 'the colonisation of the Cuban body' referring to the male sex workers in Havana). The interaction between tourists and Brazilians is rather complex because of the differences in language, social class and lifestyle. However, even these differences can be overcome. 'The gringos (foreigners) realise that they have more money, so even if they do not hire you as a prostitute, they will probably pay for food, or for your ticket to go to a show together, or your airfare and hotel if you travel together. And of course you have sex, but it is not a direct exchange, raw and naked, like you think of in prostitution. It is more of an understanding on both sides, that one has more money and can afford to pay while the other can offer other things: local knowledge and sexual pleasure. When I was younger, it was through this kind of contact that I learned a lot about human beings and about the world. Often, these relationships became very strong; I still have many friends who I met this way, who I later visited in Europe, in England, in Belgium and Italy.'[29]

Global desire   The quite different practices in this gay sub-culture, from consumer to activist, do not imply that this field cannot be called 'trans-cultural'. In spite of ideological differences, everywhere in this field you can find similar behaviour. The commitment is common in finding and experiencing homosexual relations, and sometimes in their legal recognition, but even in the last case, the desire is never far away. In this field, traditional ideas enter into discussion with more egalitarianism, in which partners in sex are perceived as equals, without domination. The rules of this game are more or less the same everywhere, although local cultural variations are possible. This field lacks a clear centre, although some regions are more peripheral than others. In Africa, south of Sahara, homosexuality officially does not exist, but the practice is different, at the same time the new constitution of South Africa Republic recognizes the rights of sexual minorities. Identification with a visible gay lifestyle is increasingly possible in more places in this world. This field lacks a professional caste, but as the Brazilians call the practicing gay 'entendidos' (initiated), one has to learn to live as a gay and it demands an initiation, a second socialisation, to find one's way in this field.

In the Muslim countries traditional ideas about gender relations and homosexuality persist. Changes occur but very slowly. Deep friendship between men as equals is appreciated, sex between males is perceived as interaction between unequals, like older – younger, active – passive.[30] The common conviction among Muslims that Koran texts should be taken literally hinders changes in spite of brave efforts of small pioneer groups.[31] In the mean time religious conviction and ''the weakness of the flesh' clash.[32]

Health care   The last trans-cultural field I would like to discuss is the rather complex field of health. Everywhere in the world, Western biomedical health care is dominant, but besides that we can find older and newer alternative systems that are influenced by the first, but sometimes clash with them. Few people know that still in the first half of the 19th century, various professionals were active in health care: besides the academic-trained physicians, also pharmacists and surgeons. The first category conquered a monopoly, based on successful developments in natural sciences in which illness was perceived as a fault in a machine that, by medical intervention, could be repaired. In 1865, Dutch Prime Minister Thorbecke approved a law that allowed practice of the medical profession only by people trained at university. All others were declared unqualified. Similar developments took place in all Western countries. Through colonialism and later development cooperation, this biomedical paradigm became dominant globally – so dominant that for many of us it is unthinkable that many other alternative ways of healing can be found that are equally effective. India knows traditional systems like adyarveda; China knows its own curative practices. In a lot of Islamic countries a medical practice existed which combined old Greek insight with practices based on the Koran. In the Punjab this system functioned so well that the English colonizers accepted this practice officially. Only much later did it become forbidden. The French colonizers had less patience with traditional healers. In most African countries, medical personnel has interiorised this disdain in such a way that it is almost impossible to speak about cooperation with traditional healers.

Let me illustrate this contempt with the story about a difficult delivery in the maternity of a hospital in Eastern Africa. A pregnant woman should have delivered already for some days, but she did not dare to give birth, as she was not wearing her amulet that could protect her against the danger of having twins. The local matron had prohibited the use of the amulet, because she was against this 'superstition'. A Western physician who was called in overruled the matron, and permitted the amulet, resulting in a successful delivery. The matron knows, of course, like everybody there, that in her country various health systems coexist: modern Western next to traditional. People use those systems alternatively. Why is this matron not more flexible? By putting herself above the traditional system, she protects her status and power. She is not the only one. The problem of the relationship between the various systems is also an actual topic in the Netherlands. With immigration, those systems are present in our country, too. Surinamese brought us the Afro-Surinamese 'winti'; with Muslim immigrants arrived the Islamic healing system. These systems offer an interesting case of a marginal cultural sub-field, far from autonomy.

Islamic healers   Through interviews and observations, Dutch anthropologist Hofer collected information on 39 Islamic healers (34 men and 5 women), all newcomers in the Netherlands.[33] He defines an Islamic healer as:

- A person who bases his or her work on an Islamic-inspired power (for example, hereditary Islamic healers (and their patients) generally healing powers said to have been passed down from the Prophet Mohammed);
- A person who retains an Islamic vision in regard to healing work;
- A person who establishes him or herself as a healer, informally (through family and friends) or formally (through advertising).hold views on certain diseases and problems that differ from those held by biomedical-trained professionals.

The Islamic healers distinguish between diseases with a natural (physical or psychological) cause and diseases with a supernatural cause. In their eyes, people consult a physician for natural diseases and go to an Islamic healer for supernatural diseases.

Islamic therapies are linked to popular belief in Islamic societies. This popular belief is made up of a mixture of elements from Islam and various important developments in the field of medicine in the Islamic world. This includes such medical traditions as Greek-inspired, Arabic-Islamic therapies, prophetic medicine with its strong influence from orthodox Islam, and biomedical therapies. An important characteristic of this popular belief is that, in addition to natural causes, supernatural causes are also regarded as possible links to disease and problems, e.g. magic, the evil eye and evil spirits (*jinns*). All sorts of therapies have developed as a result of this popular belief. Morocco and Turkey, for example, are home to a vast array of Islam-inspired therapies and healers, alongside biomedical health care. Such healers use blessings in the form of a spiritual power (*baraka*), either as an inherited gift or through faith healing using Koran verses that contain this power.

An important element in the treatments used by Islamic healers is Koran verses, which are said to have a healing effect. Koran verses are used, among other things, for faith healing and in the preparation of amulets. Most Islamic healers are of the opinion that they should not ask for money for their work, nor that they should advertise. Most of their patients come to them on the advice of relatives and friends. Moreover, it is evident that for the benefit of their own practice, they incorporate their own interpretations of the Koran and the Hadîth. Two elements constitute the basis of the legitimacy that Islamic healers attach to their work: first, the power that they use to perform their work, and second, their Islamic vision. With regard to the power, Hofer distinguishes between three types of Islamic healers: those with hereditary healing powers, those with a teacher, and those who have studied alone. In describing their personal visions, all the healers refer to passages from the Koran and the Hadîth. With regard to fees, most healers believe that no money should be charged given the religious nature of their work, although some do charge. It may be concluded, therefore, that Islamic healers view their work as being in line with Islam. This attitude is not unchallenged. Throughout time, various theological arguments have been presented from within orthodox Sunnism calling for a definition of the dividing line between Islam and popular belief. Particular emphasis is laid on the fundamentally monotheistic character of Islam. Such practices as fortune-telling, magic rituals and Saint worship are thus labeled pre-Islamic or non-Islamic. This practice can be seen as a form of symbolic struggle. They are protecting their own interests and positions. It is clear that the healers have to take into account those theological arguments. This proves that their system or field is not autonomous, but depending on religious legitimisation.

The patients   Official Islam and popular belief go hand-in-hand in everyday religious practices of many Muslims. They are not interested in theological discussions. Hofer collected information on patients of Islamic healers through interviews with 65 people, and a questionnaire distributed among 227 people. Those people had different nationalities and socio-economic backgrounds, and fell into all age categories. Eighty percent of the patients said that they had consulted a physician prior to visiting an Islamic healer. The respondents gave a variety of reasons for visiting an Islamic healer. Some were simply looking for pain relief. Others visited an Islamic healer as a result of disappointment with conventional treatment. Others were convinced that they were suffering from a supernatural disease that a physician could not treat. There was also a category of patients who consulted an Islamic healer under the motto 'It can't do any harm'. People visit Islamic healers with a variety of symptoms. Biomedically, these are physical, psychosomatic and psychological. The symptoms of most patients are chronic and non-life-threatening. One characteristic the symptoms all have in common is that they appear to be linked to situations and social problems (such as unemployment, relationships and social uncertainty) with which the person cannot cope. Some of these are existential issues, or a need for personal guidance. An important characteristic of the work carried out by Islamic healers is that they sometimes appear able to offer patients in a seemingly hopeless situation an entirely new perspective. This is done by the healer responding directly to the patient's particular situation and state of mind through a combination of symbolic acts and practical advice. This may result in the disappearance of the symptoms or the patient adopting a different attitude toward the ailments.

Islamic therapies and official health care system   In addition to their special relationship with Islam, Islamic healers are confronted with the national health care system and related services, an area which is dominated by biomedical therapies and where complementary medical practices play a secondary role. Islamic healers are also confronted with the dominant biomedical approach present in Dutch society. They respond by presenting themselves as specialists in the field of supernatural diseases, of which biomedical practitioners have no understanding. The arrival of Islamic healers has added a new dimension to the current Dutch debate on the position of complementary medicine. Given that most people who consult Islamic healers also visit physicians and other care providers, it raises the question of whether, and how, these categories of care providers should cooperate with one another. This question is especially prompted by existing, informal contacts between physicians and Islamic healers. Both factions, Islamic healers as well as physicians and other professionals, have given a variety of answers to this question. Islamic healers regard themselves as specialists in the area of the supernatural. Some Islamic healers strive in two ways to gain recognition within the Dutch health care system: either through establishing informal contacts with physicians and others or by seeking association with the network of complementary medicine.

Most of the physicians and other medical professionals who were interviewed say that they do not encourage their patients to consult Islamic healers, but they do not discourage it either. This principle is underpinned by two viewpoints. First, given therapeutic considerations, belief in supernatural forces should be taken seriously, but Islamic therapies and cooperation with Islamic healers should be rejected. Second, elements from Islamic therapies should be given a place in conventional treatments. Whenever they did mention cooperation with Islamic healers, they imposed various conditions such as reliability and openness of Islamic healers, and the fact that treatments should not conflict. These conditions imply that the near future will not see any structural cooperation between conventional and Islamic healers. However, this does not exclude mutual influence; some of the Islamic healers look for an alliance with non-religious alternative health care, like New Age forms. Biomedical professionals at least are aware of a problem, but for a lot of patients both systems are complementary.

Nationally and internationally, biomedical medicine is dominant in the field of health. The system is so dominant in the Western world that local influences are even ignored. Lately, studies in this field show that internal cultural differences exist. Feldman observed the different understanding that French and American physicians bring to Aids. In the USA, Aids is regarded as a kind of cancer, whereas in France it is conceived of as an infectious disease, like tuberculosis.[34] Alternative systems are not really challenging this dominance. It is true in the Western world that there is a growing interest in alternative approaches even among the medical establishment. Even there, doubt can be found about the effectiveness of biomedical science. However, real exchange of knowledge is not realised. The question is if it will ever be possible as long as traditional health systems depend that much on religion.

Characteristics of fields and trans-cultural fields   In this chapter I have tried to describe four trans-national cultural fields. This description was far from exhaustive, but hopefully sufficient to convince the reader that it could be useful to use this concept when analysing cultural exchange and communication today. Besides the cultural fields dealt with before, many cultural and other fields can be found in which the process of trans-nationalization can be perceived. For instance: photography (World Press Photo is a way to create a world field), management studies, audio-art, classical music, industrialised food, social sciences, some social movements like international women's organisations and anti-global movements, Afro-American religions (Winti, Umbanda, Santaria), and football, besides the growing domination of the economy as a world field, especially finances.[35] The variety of the cases mentioned shows that a common definition of field, cultural field and still more trans-cultural field is not an easy task. However, the time is right to become more precise, even if we look for open and flexible definitions. Let us make some distinctions, first between cultural and non-cultural fields, and then between national, trans-national and trans-cultural fields.

The distinction between cultural and other fields is not always easy to make. One of the reasons is that, in this stage of global capitalism, the symbolic value of an industrial product determines its value on the market, almost as much as its use value. Take cars, for instance: why does a Renault have more status than an Opel? That means that industrial production has acquired a cultural dimension. Industrial and financial fields are autonomous universes; they are not cultural fields. At the same time, the cultural industry has become more important, both economically and culturally. More cultural goods are produced industrially than ever before. 'Cultural industry' is another concept often used without a clear definition. It is characterised by economic activities in which the symbolic values of the products are central. The works of composers, writers, photographers and couturiers are counted among them. This implies that at least a lot of cultural fields also can be perceived as cultural industries. The negative consequence of this development is the possibility that the importance of the economic – of thinking in terms of profit – is becoming dominant also in the sphere of culture.[36] However, this is not a destiny, and depends on the 'actors' involved in those fields as well.

Cultural fields can be national, trans-national and trans-cultural. What are the differences? A national cultural field coincides with national borders. Trans-national cultural fields are formed by the totality of national fields. The global literary field is a good example. Pascale Casanova published a book some years ago about the global republic of literature.[37] Her view on this field implies that every national field of literature is characterised by the opposition between the pole of international writers and national writers. The poles of international writers together form the international field. In contrast, trans-cultural fields are not the result of summing up, but of exchange and mixing what results into something new; a form of 'glocalisation', i.e. local and global at the same time.

Getting back to cultural fields, they are micro-universes in which cultural goods like science, sport and music are produced, distributed and consumed and which demand of the participants in this field specific cultural capital. Also, this concept is fluid and the boundaries of its space are moving. Cultural fields have the following characteristics:

- They are structured around positions that offer more or less power, and possess more or less status. The positions in the field have more explicative power than the biography of the persons who occupy those positions.
- The development of a field depends mainly on the struggle between the unequal positions in the field, like between the established and the newcomers, both committed to the issues of the field.
- Each field demands of its actors a specific commitment, attitudes and behaviour, learned in a process of specific socialisation.
- Cultural fields are domains where the interests of the cultural producers are crucial, but they don't exist without consumers, clients and audience. These markets, especially of the fields in which cultural goods are produced industrially,

can be distinguished between the small avant-garde market of producers and a large market for a general public.

- The autonomy of field is relative. The boundaries depend on the commitment of the participants on the one hand and its recognition in the field of power on the other. When we compare those characteristics with the ones described before in the cases of trans-cultural fields, what conclusions can be drawn from these cases?
- Each trans-cultural field supposes its specific commitment with a cultural good: e.g. spiritual or corporal well-being in, respectively, the fields of religion and biomedicine, youth music in terms of pop, imaginative stories in TV drama, and all products of global cultural exchange. Based on a mix of local and global cultural idioms and/or traditions, they form new hybrid cultural systems. All forms of mixture, hybridisation and exchange can be found, especially of local and international traditions and idioms. The mergers in the cultural industry at a global scale cause a certain homogenisation; at the same time they offer new chances for locally produced goods.
- The structures of those fields vary. The fields can be structured around a dominant centre like Hollywood in the film industry or Rome in the Catholic Church. It is also possible that the field knows several power centres like football, or diffuse ones like in the gay and lesbian subculture.
- The power struggle fought in the fields between insiders, experts and newcomers conditions the development of the field. The struggle for the maintenance of existing positions or the conquest of new ones explains the dynamics of the field. The orthodoxy tries continuously to eliminate the heretics in the field of religious faith. Is a potential partner in gay subculture more interested in the common interests of the category or in individual desires? Will alternative healers ever affect the dominant position of biomedicine?
- The size of the trans-cultural fields varies. They can, as in the case of rock music or the Catholic Church, imply the whole globe or restrict themselves to several continents like football. But all autonomous fields tend to become global.
- The cultural exchange in the fields is in principle always two-way, but the exchange can at a certain moment become top

down, like in health, where biomedicine dominates. In the case of pop and rock, local idiom influences the global musical language strongly, and real exchange occurs.

- All these fields offer a possibility of identification, which transcends boundaries. They are not exclusive, but form aspects of somebody's identity as believer, as film fan or lesbian. These identities do not exclude each other; they can be combined and overlap each other. This means that today's identities are plural. The partner in communication can switch between those identities. The competence to use this plurality of identities facilitates the communication.

Intercultural communication in fields   The assumption of this study is that different social positions in social space induce different dispositions and different forms of interaction. So far we have analysed the space of everyday culture, of fields and of trans-cultural fields. What are the consequences for communication? We will look at the differences of communication between the insiders and outsiders of a field and between people inside the same trans-cultural fields with different backgrounds.

This chapter started with the experience of the special character of juridical language: the differences between an insider – the lawyer – and an outsider of this field, a dealer's girlfriend. The specific difficulty of communication between insiders and outsiders is quite common. The anthropologist Barley doing his research was another example. The problem here is not only a different view on reality, a different language, but also the distance between the people involved in the meeting. The insider often feels superior and doesn't take the outsider very seriously. This is many times the case in the communication between the medical expert and the patient. Even when talking about your own body, experts can do so with an air of superiority. Knowledge learned in a field can shock with everyday practical knowledge. Professional experts in a field can have their own blind spots, so convinced from their own better viewpoint that understanding becomes impossible. Some years ago Cardinal Simonis, the head of the RC Church in the Netherlands, was interviewed by the chief editor of the gay weekly, a well-known spokesman for the gay community. This conversation was like that between two deaf people incapable of understanding one other. Both spoke from very different fields. The gay editor spoke of homosexual desire as a form of self-realisation; the cardinal was defending the idea of sexuality as a way to procreate, because this was 'the given order of creation'.[38]

Those are all examples of communication problems. However, belonging to the same field can facilitate the communication in spite of differences in other aspects, like national, ethnic or age differences. Professionals active in the same cultural field – plastic artists, musicians, dancers, etc. – speak the same language and share the same interests and commitment. Of course they can be in competition for the same post, but that does not affect communicative competence. For professionals and experts this is obvious. However, hobbies are often rightly used as an icebreaker between strangers. But the word 'hobby' is misleading. Only if you are a real fan does it function as a bridge to understanding.

In order to illustrate how people can communicate inside a trans-cultural field, I like to use a case borrowed from a book that aims to prepare people going to Vietnam. The readers are presented with various situations and their possible reactions are evaluated. One of the proposed situations goes like this: When you, living as an 'expat', have sprained your ankle playing tennis and you want the judgment of a doctor about this injury. A friend recommends a local doctor with good knowledge of English. The doctor asks you some questions. He puts his hands on your face and asks whether the ankle is still hurting. You are surprised but answer the questions. He continues rubbing different areas of your face harder and harder. You cannot see really what is going on, but your face is hurting. The pain in your ankle seems to subside, but you are not sure whether it is because you are now more concerned about the pain in your face. Luckily, he stops and then asks you questions about your sex life, and starts explaining that a healthy sex life will maintain a healthy body. What will you do? The options presented are the following three:

- Walk out screaming that you are not homosexual.
- Glance at your watch and declare that you are late for a business meeting and that you will have to go.

- Sit and listen and make an appointment to come back with your wife as he suggests.

What would you do? For the author, 'A' is inappropriate, 'B' is acceptable and 'C' is all right if you believe in traditional Eastern forms of healing. If not, the patient has to make this clear in advance.

If we analyse the options presented in order to increase the reader's intercultural competence, we see first that this is not a case of national cultural differences. This case deals with differences in the field of health. This meeting is far less dramatic than presented. The Vietnamese doctor is underestimated: he will know of the differences between biomedical and Vietnamese traditional systems and approach the expatriate patient differently. He speaks English, so he has probably studied abroad. The expat-patient, living in Vietnam, should be aware of different medical traditions and eventually see this meeting as a chance to learn more about equally effective Vietnamese therapies.

If we imagine Islamic patients meeting care professionals in the Netherlands, it is easy to imagine communication problems. Some years ago a psychologist and an anthropologist discussed the case of a young man possessed.[39] The young boy born from Berber parents has lived since age four in the Netherlands. He has been placed in a crisis centre because of impossible behaviour at home. In the first hours after his intake, the boy shows unexplainable symptoms of pain, shakes his body and cries uncontrollably. In the days after, his situation becomes worse. Some of the Moroccan staff members and the parents think that it is an attack of the bad spirits. The psychologist interprets this behaviour as a conversion problem linked to hysteria. In his article, the psychologist presents another interpretation, equally from his professional perspective based on psychotherapy, but reinterpreting the appearance of the *Djinn (spirits)* expression of repressed sexual emotions. For this boy, spirit possession is an acceptable way to cope with traumatic experiences. The anthropologist departs from the assumption that djinns are symbols. The possession is a way to express social problems – in this case the wish of his parents who do not accept his choice of partner. All interpretations are interesting and sound more or less reasonable and confirm the knowledge of specific fields: Islamic popular ideas, psychology and symbolic anthropology. But who is right? Can they understand each other's viewpoints?

In this same light, let's look at another trans-cultural field: the gay subculture. Meeting between gays is relatively simple. Sex can become a way to bridge cultural and other differences. According to another interviewee of Parker's research, 'You may not even speak a common language, but sex itself becomes almost a form of communication. It's strange, but sex becomes a way of bridging differences, or crossing frontiers. I think that for many people there is a kind of fascination in relations with people of other places, other cultures. Through sex, cultural differences and language differences are partially wiped out: they get translated into the language of the body.'[40] It is important to be aware that communication in this subculture is not always so idyllic. Many Brazilian homosexuals have become victims of violence and murdered in cold blood. Ethnographic research[41] in Costa Rica, executed for Aids prevention, tries to explain this kind of murder. In this country, a group of youngsters called the locusts has sex with homosexuals for money and robs them, and sometimes kills them. Shifter interviewed them about their reasons for killing. Causes seem to be found in their own violent youth. The immediate reasons could be them not paying the price combined before and/or humiliation, to be pushed into a passive role that threatens their ideal of virility.

Belonging to the same field is not a guarantee of successful interaction. We remain easily linked to our everyday culture, what will interfere with the communication taking place inside and according to the rules of a specific field. Dutch Prime Minister Den Uyl and French President Mitterand, both political animals, met in The Hague. Den Uyl with his Calvinist background wanted to offer his host a typical, quick Dutch lunch with bread only, in order to save time. It became almost a political incident. Even if we share the same view on reality because people participate in the same field, in this case politics, this is no guarantee that communication will be without 'noise'. Basic everyday culture also demands its part. Eating is not related to politics but to everyday culture. Football is a trans-national sport, but at the same time a space of strong national and local feelings. In the same way, Bourdieu warns us that communication among scientists in the new international science field does not exclude ethnocentric and national interests. The reader will remember the fight between USA and French scientists about the discovery of the HIV virus a decade ago. Trans-cultural fields are mergers of local and global elements, so they can function as a bridge or impediment for cultural understanding, depending on the emphasis put on one or both origins. One thing we know for sure is that if we don't take into account trans-cultural fields such as communication context, effective communication will be very difficult.

In this chapter, we have seen how fields are specific spaces of cultures next to the more local everyday culture and function as context of intercultural communication. We have seen, too, how those fields under influence of globalisation tend to become trans-cultural. In the next chapter I will retake the local global tension from the perspective of consumption. Does a global lifestyle exist everywhere? And what are the implications for communication?

Notes

1. Alfred Schutz (1964) *Collected papers I & II*. The Hague, Martinus Nijhof.

2. Pierre Bourdieu (1997) *Meditations Pascaliennes*. Paris Seuil, p.171

3. Bourdieu. O.c. p.178.

4. For a critical analysis of Barley's study, see: Janet L. Roitman: Lost innocence; the production of truth and desire in Northern Cameroon in: *Critique of Anthropology* 14/4 1994: pp 315-334.

5. Nigel Barley (1986) Ceremony; an anthropologist misadventures in the African Bush. New York, Holt & Co: p. 83.

6. Barley o.c. p.107.

7. B. Lahire (1998) *L'Homme pluriel*. Paris, Nathan.

8. Norbert Elias (1991) *Mozart de sociologie van een genie*. Amsterdam, Van Gennep.

9. Goran Ahrne (1994). London, Sage.

10. Compare Ch. Handy. (1990) *Inside organization* BBC Books, 1990. Fons Trompenaars, (1993). *Riding the waves of culture*. London, The economist books.

11. See among others: Pierre Bourdieu (2000) *Les structures sociales de l'économie*; postcriptum: du champ national au champ international. Paris, Seuil. Pp 271-281.

12.This supremacy is the reason why other forms of economy, based on exchange, are not recognised any more. Family economy or economy of gifts are not recognised as autonomous forms of economy.

13. Pierre Bourdieu. (1996) *Sur la television* . Paris, Liber Editions.

14. D. Marchetti (2002) International images in: *Actes de la Recherche en Sc.Soc*. n. 2002.

15. N. Vink (1988). *The telenovels and emancipation*. Amsterdam, KIT Publishers.

16. Manuel Castels (1997) *The power of identity*. Oxford, Blackwell.

17. Motti Regev (1997) Rock esthetics and musics of the world. In: *Theory, Culture & Society* 14/3 pp.125-142.

18. Krister Malm and Roger Wallis (1992) *Media, policy and music activity*. London/ New York, Polity.

19. *Time,* 13-11-2000.

20. Mario d'Angelo 1998) L'impitoyable industrie du disque. In: *Le monde Diplomatique* Juin 1998.

21. Bart Hofstede (2000) *Nederlandse cinema wereldwijd*. Amsterdam, Boekmanstichting.

22. Hofstede o.c. p.24.

23. Nestor Garcia Canclini (1997) *Consumidores y ciudadanos*: conflitos multi-culturales de la globalizacion. Mexico, Grijalbo.

24. Esi Dogbe (2003) Elusive modernity; Portraits of the city in popular Ghanaian videos. In: Paul Tiyambe Zeleza and Casandra Rachel Veney. *Leisure in Urban Africa*. Trenton/Asmara, Africa World Press. 227-248.

25. Joao Silverio Trevisan (1986*) Devassos no paraiso*. Sao Paulo, Max Limonad; Helio Silva (1993)Travesti; a invencao do feminine. Rio, Dumara; Richard Parker (1999*). Beneath the equator.* Cultures of desire; male homosexuality and emerging gay communities in Brazil. New York/London, Routledge

26. Richard Parker (1999). P.55.

27. Peter Fry (1982) *Para o ingles ver*. Rio, Zahar.

28. Parker o.c.

29. Parker o.c. p. 199.

30. See; Arno Schmitt and Jehoeda Schofer (1990) *Sexuality and eroticism among males in Müslim societies*. New York/London/ Norwood, Harrington Press.

31. Omar Nahas (2003) *Islam en homosexualiteit*. Amsterdam/Utrecht, Uitgeverij Bulaaq/Yoesuf.

32. If a gay tourist has sex with a local partner in a Muslim country such as Tunisia, then that is done in the dark because, according to Islamic prescription, men do not show their bodies between navel and knee to others!

33. For the following summary of Hofer's study, I have used from the Internet: summary.chofer.nl.muslimhealers by the author.

34. Quoted by Kaja Finkler. Diffusion reconsidered; Variation and transformation in biomedical practice. In: *Medical Anthropology*. 19/2 pp 1-39.

35. Bourdieu mentions that the learned fields become trans-national and that an international community of scholars is forming itself, in Bourdieu (1997).

36. Both Bourdieu (2001) and Canclini (2002) defend the thesis that the cultural industries are too important to be left only in the hands of the market; international legislation is, in their opinion, needed.

37. Pascale Casanova (1999) *La republique internationale des lettres*. Paris, Le Seuil.

38. Gaykrant 22/9/2000.

39. L.E.E.Ligthart (1996) Jnun en ernstig getraumatiseerde Marokkaanse joneren in: *Medische Antropologie* 8/1 1996 pp.55-68 and E. Bertels Jnun als symbol een reactie in Idem pp.69-77.

40. Parker o.c. p.200.

41. Jacobo Schifter (2000) *Public sex in a Latin American Society*. New York/London/Oxford, Haworth Hispanic/Latino Press.

Chapter 5

SITY AND DIFFERENCES

The idea of a global culture that brings an end to differences between national cultures and even between groups is rather popular among journalists and bestseller authors writing on globalisation. They elaborate ideas like the 'Disneyisation' of society[1] or 'McDonaldisation' of the world, meaning that this fast food enterprise becomes a metaphor for the homogenization of cultures. This image implies for its inventor Ritzer[2] that in the world a process of rationalisation is going on, influencing all aspects of human existence from birth to death. All human activities everywhere will be organised on the basis of efficiency, calculability, control and predictability, like hamburgers are. Recently, however, Ritzer[3] distanced himself from his own ideas and recognised that this approach does not take into account the complexity of the global economy. It is true that apparently uniform patterns of consumption can be found in many places of the world, as in food habits and dress, but to what extent does this represent a global culture? The last chapter about trans-cultural fields emphasised a certain homogenisation of the world. What about the cultural differences; where can we find them? Only at the level of everyday cultures? Or between the fields? This chapter will show existing differences in the world which go farther than the diversity of lifestyles made possible through mass consumption.

I continue with the distinction made earlier between everyday life culture and cultural fields. In the first place, I will examine if we can find a global cultural pattern affecting everyday culture worldwide. It is true that the consumption of industrialised goods is increasingly becoming today's way to present one's personality, in which differences in dressing, body care and housing play an important role. Diversity is growing. However, the difference between the poor and the rich in the world remains a very important intervening factor – a difference that reaches deeper than variation in lifestyles. Another difference of another nature, but also related to everyday culture, is the way in which believers and agnostics or secular people shape their daily routine. What can be the influence of faith on the believer's daily life?

The second part of this chapter examines how far-reaching the globalisation of fields is. Are fields everywhere trans-cultural and a real context for communication? Or do differences still exist here too? I will show that the hierarchy between the fields existing in the Western world is quite different from the hierarchy existing in Africa, for example, where economy is not dominating, but building relations as part of human exchange is at least equally important. In the Western world, not everyone shares the dominant vision; the anti-globalist movement also defends alternative views on the world.

Culture and consumption   Spring 2004 football player David Beckham was in the news worldwide, when, having signed a 40-million-dollar contract with Gillette to promote their razors, a woman revealed that he had been unfaithful to his wife Victoria Adams. It is not clear which of the two news items attracted more media attention, but both were related. Beckham has become an icon, a public image that is a product in itself with a high value. With the help of his wife, ex-pop singer and expert in marketing, Beckham has constructed an image not so much of a skilled football player, but of a sex symbol, popular with young girls and gay men all over the world. Beckham is continuously busy with his public image, by changing his outlook, hairstyle, dress and preference of cars, among other things. All those items are discussed in detail by the media. Beckham is typical not only of a merger between sport and commercialisation of sport images, but of a more general trend toward working on self-presentation and image building – in essence, the idea that we become what we consume.

In earlier phases of capitalism, one's status was measured by his/her position in the production process; increasingly a person's lifestyle and consumption pattern matter as indicators of status. Work as vocation and self-realisation has become a privilege of the elite, according to Bauman. Where as before the ethos of work was dominant, now the aesthetics of consumption prevails. Consumption has become a ritual and demands more time. Exemplary is the different role of shopping, implying a lot more than satisfying a household's basic needs. Everywhere in the Western world, as well as in industrialising countries shopping centres and malls arise, symbols and temples at the same time of consumer rituals aimed at self-realisation and self-presentation.

To become an icon is very exclusive and, therefore, not for everybody. Many people, nonetheless, feel a lot of pressure to improve their own self-image. A traditional way to improve self-image has been fashion, characteristically perceived as a woman's concern. Increasingly, men's fashion is catching up, passing through a lot of changes in the last decades following changes in self-image and perception of men's social position – a development that can be summarised schematically in the following three phases[4]. The classic dark suit expressed the male patriarchal authority over wife and children. The patriarch wanted distance and demanded obedience and respect. The only emotion these men could show was anger, because of the transgression of rules they were responsible for. That was the role as father and boss. At the end of the sixties, the ethics of self-development comes in vogue for men and women. Men's appearance becomes more informal. Hippy dress with loose Indian-style shirts and jeans sets the trend. Equality between people and the sexes turns into the ideal and differences in power are denied. In the last decade of the 20th century, the situation changes again. Aiming at equality becomes old-fashioned. Differences in power according to the dominant opinion are a reality and, in an organisation, even a necessity. The boss is superior. However, the boss cannot behave in the same authoritarian way as before. The aspiration for more democratic relations has not disappeared completely. An effective boss should motivate and delegate. The man plays a role now, without showing that it is a performance. This feeling expresses itself in lively-coloured ties and shirts, but for the rest he remains, in function, formally dressed. Power, after all, should be visible in the 'power-suit'.

In the inter-ethnic relation in many countries of Western Europe, the veil and Islamic fashion are another way of expressing identity. Scarves covering the hair and long coats and dresses form a particular style that indicates that the wearer wants to be a Muslim, a conscious Islamic woman. She wants to be different but at the same time belong to a group. This happens with differences in consumption – they are used to visualise the individual's identity, but often this is at the same time a collective identity. This aim is sometimes achieved in such a way that a Muslim woman once angrily remarked, 'Dutch people are so indifferent; they do not even ask me about the reasons for my veil.'

Lifestyle, social class and identity   Social differences between people are expressed often in lifestyles, clusters of consumptive behaviour specific for segments of markets and target groups, not clearly related to class. Apparently, consumption has made society more democratic. Everyone can drive a car if they want to. Jeans are worn in all layers of society, as the distinction between high and low cultural products seems to be erased. At the same time, the possibilities to distinguish oneself have increased. Lifestyle is sometimes used to replace social class, suggesting that class differences are disappearing. Marketing experts and politicians, inclusively social democrats, avoid the use of this category. The Netherlands is, in their view, a democratic society where the market gives us the same opportunities and influence. Of course there are small differences, but of minimal interest. I agree with the fact that social class is not the only basis of distinction, but we are far from an equal society. Granted, car driving *is* possible for everyone, but the make of car you drive still marks you. In a similar vein, the number of students entering university, including females and immigrants, has increased considerably, but their participation in the academic ranks is far from proportional. Taste classifies us and is related to our social position as men or women, whether working with hand or head, or as citizen or 'illegal', etc. We have seen that before. What matters here is to emphasise that the variation in lifestyles has consequences for the identity of the consumer living and participating in different social spaces – in everyday culture and fields.

Identities are plural. People are not always the same. They can assume different identities here and there, and change between then and now. They can assume different appearances, and with dress and other aspects of self-presentation, ego changes too. In an interview about the supermarket of styles that is our society, an Amsterdam student describes the daily practice.

'Life is a role play. You change all the time. From eleven till five I am a student. Later I am a flirting woman strolling in the Vondel Park. Visiting my parents I become a daughter. In the disco I am somebody else again. All those different roles also demand different dress codes.'

This flexibility – which creates real despair for marketing experts – has instigated the expression 'flexi-style'. It implies that for the presentation of self, non-verbal communication – lifestyles based on dress and body care – become increasingly more important. In other words, you are not what you say, but what you appear to consume. This results in the plurality of identities. But the root of this plurality of self is an idea generally accepted in our society: a new common sense idea about what a human being really is. This concept can be best explained by analysing what is called 'the new middle class'.[5]

The development of the post-fordist production has resulted in a huge number of specialists working in the production, circulation and marketing of symbolic goods. The social change in our society is not any more dependent on the working class or political and economic elite. Other groups set the tone and determine the trends. Meant are not the yuppies (young urban professionals) or similar categories in the jargon of marketing people. A lot more is at stake than just patterns of consumption in the culture of Western societies. A new progressive middle class plays a crucial role, different from the traditional sectors of the 'petite bourgeoisie', and a consequence of changes in the production process, like the importance of knowledge and information. Traditional middle class occupied the position between workers and the managing elite. A small segment worked independently in the so-called 'free professions'. The new middle class is active mainly in the production and distribution of symbolic goods. They are mainly cultural intermediaries active in publicity, marketing, mass media and advertising, or they are employed as helpers stimulating others to achieve a better and healthier lifestyle, like therapists, relationship counsellors and management advisors.

This progressive middle class presents a mentality other than the traditional one.[6] It has abandoned the narrow asceticism of the old small bourgeoisie, which postpones enjoying life now in favour of later. The actual device is the realisation of self, here and now – a change from the ethos of obligation to the ethos of pleasure. The adepts of the later ethos work with passion on the project of self-realisation; they see life for all as the development of their own personality. They are very fit to work in the symbolic organisation of consumption, stimulating, orienting and 'improving' people's tastes. This kind of idea can easily be found in advertisements like in this slogan for source water: 'You drinks what you are!' Another example is the way in which a huge Dutch warehouse advertises blazers: 'In balance with yourself. … Fashion as self-expression. It gives you a possibility to give form to every mood, surprising yourself. You have to assume a viewpoint. The individual today is defined through the decisions made and which make up his or her identity.'[7] It is no coincidence that the same model of the rational decision-maker is used for marketing as in the economy. The new middle class, although its discourse seems sometimes opposed or even subversive, is the natural ally of the dominant classes, legitimising their lifestyle as a model.[8]

The new middle class has abandoned the ascetic attitude, but this doesn't imply losing self-control. On the contrary, this is stricter than ever. Watch, for instance, how these people cope with time, in spite of all domestic tools they have at their disposal and intended to make daily life easier. As it turns out, they have less time available than ever before – yet with so many opportunities available, and so many at the same time! With both parents responsible for the education of their children, for example, every effort is be made to secure the development of an all-round personality. A consequence of this educational ideal is the perceived need to stimulate and organise sport, a host of extra-curricular classes, as well as time to visit friends. Today's parents need rather complicated schedules to manage such a household. At the same time, they need to make choices such as those between their own development and those of their partners and children. Because two wage earners are often involved, they have more opportunities than ever but not more time. They live like people with a constant agenda in their heads and a ticking internal clock.

Control in terms of self reaches farther. With a service-oriented mentality as a condition for being successful in one's profession today, making a career supposes a spontaneous control of one's own emotions. Another condition is maintaining control over one's emotions in interactions with colleagues and at home. We have mentioned already the interesting study conducted by Eva Illouz, who sees emotion as a form of cultural capital. To be a competent communicator is not only demanded from politicians and managers on the work floor, but also a skill demanded in personal relations, certainly for middle class members, because it is their main capital. Improving one's self in everyday culture and in professional fields is a common exigency; even free time is used for the realisation of self. One illustration of this trend is the increase of visits to museums by the middle class. At the same time, spare time is lived as a utopia, as free choice. Of course this ideal is never achieved. Living one's life as a project that can and should be improved continuously is a concept that is spreading all over the world. However, it remains characteristic for the higher and middle class and increasingly for the working class in Western Europe. The poor of this world have other, more immediate preoccupations.

Cultural gaps   Nobody better than Nancy Scheper Hughes has shown how big the distance can be between our middle-class concepts and the reality of the poor as she has in her beautiful study *Death without Weeping*.[9] Scheper-Hughes has worked first among poor families in northwestern Brazil for the Peace Corps and later did research, in the same place, as an anthropologist. She describes very honestly how she was shocked by the indifference of the poor mothers about the death of their very young children: no weeping and no other signs of grief. For the author, such a death would have been a drama of great impact. Why did the mothers react with indifference, without showing emotions? How is this possible? The scholar asked herself: what kind of mothers are these that they do not show emotion and grief? It took her long years of communicating with the women to discover the truth. The women are far from indifferent, but because of their extreme poverty – more concretely a lack of sufficient and healthy food for their children – they have learned a strategy of survival. They make a distinction between active children struggling for life and the passive ones, who 'don't want to live'. The mothers avoid emotional involvement with the children until their second year because the probability they will die is too great and the emotional costs too high. Once this secret was revealed, Scheper Hughes became more shocked at the indifference of society and institutions like State and Church that seemed to ignore the high child mortality – no official data was even available! This is an extreme case but, in a situation where the poor seem to participate in mass consumption, the question remains as to whether it has the same meaning for everyone.

Miscommunication between rich and poor occurs also in our own society. A shocking example of miscommunication has been analysed in a PhD thesis on homeless and drug addicts.[10] Author Geeske Hoogenboezem found that people who need professional help the most are excluded from it. Why? Most professionals suppose in their care-taking that each client is an autonomous individual, capable of making his or her own decisions about their future, and that the client can stick to the rules, according to the dominant model we have just analysed. This is not true in the case of this group. The researcher asked the interviewees to tell their life stories according to topics like youth, career, relations and plans for the future. Most of them finished their stories in three minutes. They told isolated incidents about a friend, about losing their homes, but without any overview or chronology. In essence, they do not have a grip on their life stories or their lives. It is very difficult for them to appear at appointments and, for that reason, they are considered to be irresponsible persons and are excluded from help, while the few clients with coherent life stories and realistic plans for the future are the ones who receive the most help. In spite of good intentions, this is a dramatic example of miscommunication.

Consumption in the south   It is enough to watch TV to become aware that major parts of the world population do not participate in the so-called society of consumption. Industrially produced goods are not available for everybody in the world in the same way. Differences in access are quite conspicuous and structured according to one's position in society. Cars are still available only for a minority, but household tools like plastic buckets, CD's or cigarettes are available for the poor majority. You can buy cigarettes in Ouagadougou, capital of the poor Burkina Faso, for 50 CFA a piece (less than five euro cents) and so they become available for the poor young boys without employment who want to participate in modern life. As a further example, the beauty product line of Avon has set up a network of saleswomen in Brazil among the lower income women. They sell their products on a freelance basis in slums and far away in the countryside. But the participation in consumption of industrial products is more complicated, as a comparative study among poor and middle-class households in Santiago, the capital of Chile, will show.[11]

Despite significant economic progress recently, Chile remains a country with a high level of poverty. Poor residents who live in shantytowns in Santiago are under pressure to evacuate the valuable land they occupy. Besides enduring the hardships of material poverty, the poor must face a society that looks down upon them.

'Just because we are small, just because we are black, just because we go around with few and simple clothes that, even though they are clean,… but I mean just because we live in a shantytown… there is a lot of discrimination.'[12]

The poor are aware of their social stigmatisation and, for that reason, they try to establish a social distance within this category. Analysing the conversations among Chileans from upper/middle and lower income sectors gives an insight into the position of the poor. For many, poverty is perceived as natural – no need for the higher income groups to feel responsible for their situation.

'The problem is that poverty is like leprosy… the whole world has had that leprosy since the days of Jesus' Christ. And 'somebody has to do the dirty work.'[13]

This is the natural way of society, and more and more the poor are blamed for being in that situation. Opinion has it that they either lack the willpower, the discipline or the work ethic to successfully commit to a job and to overcome their impoverished condition. It is hardly surprising that people make an effort not to be classified as poor.

'I would say that ...how I could define it..'middle-middle'. Middle...not high not low, I mean, middle... for the common Chilean. A level in which most of us are, I think, right?' [14]

In an attempt to avoid being classified as poor, people regard material possessions as playing a key role. People in Chile indulge in conspicuous consumption in order to earn respect and to cultivate a sense of identity and self-esteem.

'If you are not part of the fashion or you don't wear what is in fashion, you are looked down upon. So you have no choice.'

Among lower income groups in Chile, consumer goods convey that the owner is not poor. Having access to colour TV or stereo equipment is surely a step in alleviating the stigma of being poor. Since wages are so low that poor people cannot save money to purchase such equipment, credit emerges as the only alternative. Contrary to what middle and high-income groups believe, people in debt know that goods bought on credit are more expensive. Consumption on credit appears to be a personal way of bridging the gap between rich and poor, in other words,

'In order to rise (!), you have to get into debt.' 'People rely on credit because it is the only alternative in order to rise in 'status', to have a little more.'

Again, what is for the poor a rational solution, to go into debt, is for the middle class and richer proof of their lack of education and their passive surrender to the market.

In the capital of the neighbouring country during the last decade, an urban transformation took place that introduced the ideal of neo-liberal consumption to the redesign of the cityscape of Buenos Aires. This urban transformation legitimised at the same time the unequal relation between Argentina and the USA, as between elite and middle class and the rest of the population. Emanuela Guano [15] explains in a fascinating article what this redesign means for the everyday of the population – the shift in spatial organisation implied in a privatisation of public space, which was correlated with the privatisation of public services. The new spaces, i.e. malls, citadels and theme parks, became new, semi-public space with two characteristics. On the one hand they function as showcases of a consumption society and, on the other hand those spaces control their visitors and exclude the poor. Although those spaces exclude the 'dangerous' lower classes, they address the middle-class public, affected by neo-liberal politics but still politically undecided. The first shopping mall was constructed in the early 90s and impressed the Portenos [16] as self-enclosed, sanitized structures devoted to consumption. The visual and spatial experience of vicarious consumption stimulated the desire of the middle class to be included in this world of modernity. Guano gives the behaviour of Beatriz as an illustration of how many Portenos use the downtown malls. Beatriz, an accountant in her late forties who freelances from home after she lost her job, goes to the mall almost every weekend. She does not buy anything because she cannot afford it with the possible exception of a hamburger at McDonald's for her son. But she enjoys window-shopping. To her, a trip to the mall is like reading one of those fashion magazines replete with European and North American designer clothes. But the mall is more fun, Beatriz adds,

'Because you get to walk right through the displays; you don't just see them, but you get to feel them and even try them on.' [17]

The distance in consumption patterns between rich and poor is even stronger elsewhere. *The New Rich in Jakarta* is an ethnographic study by Lizzy van Leeuwen. [18] During Soeharto's new economic order, a new middle class has developed with a lifestyle in which the rich jog before work, alternate eating fast food and health food, and watch soaps at night. They buy mostly imported products in malls and supermarkets, certainly not at the local market. They live in separate quarters and move around in their cars, avoiding direct contact with the excluded masses of the population. The use of industrialised modern products also implies second-hand goods.

Karen Hansen has researched the international trade in second-hand clothes. In her opinion, it's not just a matter of a commodity like second-hand cars but one that illustrates how in Africa the local and the West interact. She is convinced of the pivotal role of clothing in the very process of making African men and women consumers, although in a different way and time. She found an export worth 1.5 billion dollars in 1995 from the industrialised world to mainly Africa, south of the Sahara. Exporting countries are: United States, Germany, the Nether-lands, Belgium, and the United Kingdom. In Zambia, all layers of the population surprisingly use those clothes; class and income distinctions are not very marked. People buy these garments not just for economic reasons, i.e. their price, but they also play a role in the general desire to participate in the modern world. For that reason, they have to be authentic, really second-hand. In terms of fashion, 'the latest' plays an important role, especial-ly for young people. Those imported garments mean more style for those who wear them. Using those clothes is not enough; crucial is the style of wearing them, determined by local ideas about what is elegant and fashionable. A modern, fashionable appearance has become for the *Sapeurs*, a group of youth from the Congo, a goal in itself. They travel to Paris and Brussels look-ing for an identity as winners, in which dressing up is crucial. [19]

Research among Pentecostalists in Ghana revealed a pecu-liar and ambivalent attitude in relation to consumer goods, like clothes. [20] Commodities from the global market are represented as enchanted by Satan's demons, and consumption as a battle-field where the war between devil and God takes place. Yet, there is no advice to believers to abstain from the consumption of all imported goods, but the Pentecostalist discourse empha-sises the risks and dangers imbued in commodities and at the same time, present itself as the sole instance which is able to handle the impact of globalisation.

Alienation or creativity?   How do we interpret this spread of consumer goods and consumption patterns all over the globe? Since the sociologists of the Frankfurter Schule have analysed the cultural industry in the thirties of the last century, many negative things have been said about mass consumption, which should lead to superficiality and alienation. Indeed, it is easy to discover negative elements in the so-called society of consumers. It is enough to remember the waste of energy and resources implied. The damage for the environment is difficult to estimate. The restriction imposed by the ecological limits to economic growth imply that increasing the level of consumption by the poor would be impossible without a change of the actual lifestyles of the privileged groups in the world. A small country like the Netherlands is living far above its possibilities. We use, by importing food from elsewhere, fifteen times more of the space of the world than is justified by the national borders.

However, consuming is not just alienation. Let us look also at the bright side – that means not looking at it from a macro-perspective, but from the perspective of everyday life. Based on intensive research of the British youth culture, Paul Willis puts the doom scenario by the Frankfurter Schule behind him. With lot of examples, he argues that especially the young consumers are actively involved in making sense of their lives and constructing their own identities by their way of coping with cultural goods. Willis calls this 'symbolic work and symbolic creativity'. One of his arguments is the active way that pop music is used; it implies a lot more than passively listening to the 'top ten'. The very selection of your own preferred pieces out of what's in production today, and still more from the last fifty years, supposes a lot of work. Visit a record shop and watch, says Willis, how intensively young people are involved in comparing lists of music, listening to the records and making their choice. They use today's technology like tape-recorders, VD and the Internet to link their own personal collections. Anyway, listening to music supposes creativity of the consumer; it has to become your own music. Intensive listening to records and CDs, writing down the text and memorising the words, help to appropriate music in a meaningful way. And of course it is not a solipsist activity; music is also used to make clear to others one's own feelings.

The same active attitude can be noticed in coping with fashion, watching TV and film, and reading reviews. In Willis's opinion, all this leads to grounded aesthetics. This is different from the traditional way that a typical visitor to a museum enjoys art: from a distance. Grounded aesthetics implies touching, manipulating, using, discussing dancing – far from the elitist vision on art.

'We are seeing a shift from the brilliant enlightenment of the few
to a dusky, sometimes disturbing, lightening of the many.'[21]

Willis is convincing in his plea to perceive mass consumption by youth in a positive perspective.

Earlier, Canclini tried in his study *Consumidores y Ciudadanos*[22] to understand how the changes in patterns of consumption have transformed the possibilities and forms to exercise citizenship in Latin America.[23] Canclini defends the thesis that popular participation in today's society is achieved not via political means, like elections and political parties, but via participation in the market of consumer goods, especially cultural goods distributed by the mass media, like soaps and series. Consumption was traditionally perceived by Latin American intelligentsia as alienation – something very negative or at least superficial, not worthwhile to take into account. Political participation was the final goal of all popular organisations. During the economy of import substitution, the opposition between national and imported products has been a crucial theme; national defence against imperialism, economic and cultural, was needed. But, Canclini states, times have changed radically. Today such approach would be without sense. Culture now is a process of multinational assembling; cars, for example, are produced not just in one country but also in many places, and assembled somewhere else. This is true not only for industrial products, but even more for cultural goods – products of cultural hybridisation. A Mexican film like *Como Agua Para Chocolate* and the Brazilian *Dona Flor e Seus Dois Maridos,* very popular in their own and the international market, could become hits 'because they combined references of their own identity and the cultural internationalisation of these countries.'[24]

Canclini thinks that in Latin America, under the influence of globalisation, identity is also redefined. Identity is not any more organised by participation in specific, mostly mono-linguistic territories – nations structured by the logic of the state –

but by participation in trans-national communities of consumers, like the fans of rock-music or football. He sees a transition from modern identities based on the nation state to post-modern identities because of people participating in 'trans-national communities' constructed mainly through the media. Canclini stresses the cultural integration of the continent in the world market of cultural goods. Of course he knows that this integration is not the same for everybody. Class continues to play an important role. He distinguishes between three different cultural circuits. The mass of the population has limited its incorporaton in the global culture by its exclusive access to radio and TV. Some minority groups of popular and middle classes could become more informed citizens via access to cable TV and video. Only a small portion of the entrepreneurial elite has access to the third circuit of fax, email and parabolic antennas.

Canclini and Willis offer strong arguments for a positive view on emerging consumption patterns. However, this is only one side of the coin. Next to this active and identity construction side, we should be aware of its individualist character. We have seen in the case of the Chilean poor that consumption is their way to resolve their marginal position. Unfortunately, this is not an exception, but the rule. Consuming appears to seduce everyone to perceive personal happiness as the solution for structural problems like exclusion and stigmatisation. People perceive only individual solutions instead of structural ones. This is one of the reasons that politics and social mobilisation have lost their appeal. In many parts of the world, particularly in Europe and Latin America, it has become more difficult to mobilise people to improve their social position or to defend collective interests, as is often the expectation of leftist, middle-class activists.

We may conclude that consuming goods has become a very important aspect of most people's everyday lives. It is a way of constructing their identity. However, appearance should not mislead us. Depending on the continent – Africa, Latin America, Asia, or the Pacific – and the degree its economy has been integrated in global capitalism, consumption has different meanings and can transmit different messages. Participating in global consumption seems possible for everyone today, but it is the prerogative of middle and higher classes all over the world to share and practice the idea of a personality as a life project. This is the basis of a global consumption culture that creates diversity and excludes at the same time the poor as the 'others', incapable of corresponding to the middle-class norms.

Religion and everyday culture   Another cultural difference which can make communication difficult is the gap between common sense religiosity of societies where religion and culture are mixed and others, like in Western Europe, where religion is not absent but has became a private matter without influence on everyday life. No doubt that in the Netherlands religion has lost its importance, not only in public life, but also in the everyday life of the people. Neither religion nor religious norms orient their daily practice. For most Dutch people living in a society where religion penetrates and shapes everyday life, it is very difficult to understand. What do they answer if people ask if they believe in God? How do they relate to people who frequently use expressions like '*Si Dios quiere*' or '*Imshallah*' ('If God wants it')? What does religion mean, for example, in the daily life of poor West-African women?

A case study   I have been participating in research undertaken by the Royal Tropical Institute where, by listening to what Muslim women say about how religion is experienced in their everyday lives. The research has sought to understand how women operate within their own context to empower themselves and justify their claims.[25] It is within this context that the term 'Muslim women' needs to be understood. The use of this term was not intended to homogenise what are, in reality, very different life situations. Instead, it acknowledges that Islam may be a dominant part of the cultural setting that is interpreted in different ways. Listening to people makes it possible to distinguish the way in which religion becomes part of the set of cultural significations, how it is experienced in everyday life and how women use their understanding of religion to justify their claims on society.

Fieldwork was undertaken in three different sites in Mali – in a rural village, in a rural town, and in a slum of the capital. The research in Senegal was carried out in two rural villages, centres of, respectively, Mourides and Bay Fal brotherhoods, and in two urban slums of Dakar. The differences between the rural and urban sites and the two countries proved to be relatively small. The most interesting conclusion from re-reading the interviews is that women, although perceived as poor by the interviewers, do not identify themselves as such. They do mention hardship and deprivation, and lack of means and possibilities, but they do not use 'poor' as a category to describe themselves. Two times during focus group discussions the women started to talk about the problems of the community in order to get help from the interviewers, but even then they did not identify themselves as poor. This is different from situations in Latin America where women readily talk in terms of 'we the poor' … the 'exploited against they' … the ' immoral rich'. In contrast, the poor women in Mali and Senegal do not feel exploited, nor do they see a common interest in opposing other social groups.

About women as believers, the research found the following. There is not one Muslim identity; rather there are various identities. There are differences at the level of religious organisations active in the religious field, but also differences between what Islam means in the daily life of poor women and their everyday culture. From their perspective, religion means three things: it lends meaning to their lives, it provides moral rules, and it facilitates community building. Muslim women can identify themselves in their personal religious experience with one of these functions or a combination of them.

Islam is first and foremost about faith and *personal contact with God.* Many women spoke about how their faith empowers them to cope with the struggles of daily life and the hardships that they experience. What is striking is the way in which many women talk about their faith. Devotion to God – faith in Allah – is integral to their daily life. Many interviews are imbued with assertions of faith and a personal relationship with God.

'God brought us into this world to worship Him.' *(Interview in Dakar, Senegal).*

Women see their religion as spiritual development, as a way of communicating with God, which gives meaning to their life and consolation in dealing with problems. Allah is represented as an understanding, forgiving, merciful and just God, who consoles those who suffer.

'Islam gives me much strength. Faith in God helps me to have the strength to overcome problems. When you have problems you have to turn to God always.' *(Married woman, 37, Touba, Senegal)*

Religion helps Muslim women to accept situations in their lives over which they have no control or in which they do not have a choice, such as poverty, being in a polygamous relationship or childlessness. The belief that God decides their fate helps women to accept the situations they live in.

'My life is in God's hands. Everything in my life is up to Him. I am poor. I accept it. Only God can make people rich.' *(Married woman, Banamba, Mali)*

Muslim women believe that God is just and merciful. He will compensate them for the hardship they experience now. Those women who live under difficult circumstances say that religion gives them peace and supports them when they feel bad. In such a case, they pray and ask God for help.

'Islam helps a lot in my life, especially when I have a problem; I turn to Islam for help. When I have a problem I do my ablutions, I pray to God, and I ask Him to help me.' *(Married woman Dakar, 19)*

However, the acceptance of one's fate as God's will does not mean fatalism. A good Muslim must work for his or her survival. Certainly, this is the conviction of the members of the Mouride order. For them, sanctification is achieved by working for the community and/or their spiritual leaders.

Secondly, religion gives the believer a code of conduct, a moral framework for how to live in society as a good person. Islam offers an ethical and moral code that guides behaviour and regulates social relationships. Common to the diverse sites at which the fieldwork was conducted was the assertion that being a Muslim means having faith in God, praying, fasting, helping the poor and behaving in a manner that is charitable and neighbourly. Certainly for Muslims these constitute the central tenets of the five pillars of Islam, and thus are widely known and referred to. This is not unique in itself. What is unique is the latter assertion – helping the poor and behaving in a manner that is charitable and neighbourly – which takes different forms in different cultures. In Mali as well as in Senegal among the poorest groups, this is translated into 'having solidarity with the poor'. Solidarity with other people means giving money and food to people in need and sharing whatever you have with poor people in your neighbourhood, even if you were poor yourself.

For the Muslims, this moral code also includes the many prohibitions and restrictions cited regarding dress, sexual behaviour, gender roles and relations, and food and drink – all of which pertain to the proper behaviour of a real Muslim wife. Women, especially the elder ones, said that wearing decent clothes was part of religious practice. They said that good Muslim women should cover their hair and wear long skirts (*pagnes*) and loose shirts; only the hands, face and feet can be uncovered. Women should not wear clothes that might seduce men. Clothing has its own meaning and can identify people, especially women, as believers. Religion tells men and women to control their instincts and not to have sex outside marriage. Women should not say bad things about other people, nor say negative things in general or raise their voices in any instance. Women say that religion tells them to obey their parents and husbands, and to take care of the children and the household work. All these rules are, of course, highly normative, and it is almost impossible for a woman to follow them all the time. Women are aware of this; they say they want to live according to the Islamic rules but sometimes they have to break them in order to survive. Several interviewees insisted on the fact that following the Islamic moral code is very difficult, especially for young people, and especially in the capital cities. To start a relation with a married man, a 'sugar daddy', is for some girls an immoral but tempting way to participate in the world of modern consumption.

This ethical side of religion – obedience to the rules – is even more important in the case of the Bay Fal. Their rules are even further personalised. God's will becomes clear in the wishes of the particular sheik that the believer is following. Bay Fal are known to be submissive because they call themselves 'the servants of the Mourids'. In their world, obedience is very important, and they are known to follow without questioning the orders of their spiritual leaders, the *serignes* and *khalifes*. This is how a young woman puts it:

'I will never go against my serigne's will, no matter how hard it is going to be for me to follow it. You always do what your serigne asks you to do.' *(Unmarried girl, 18, Darou Khafor)*

For members of the Bay Fal brotherhood, one cannot be a Muslim without a *serigne*; a Muslim should follow his orders, and it is only in this case that she/he can become a *talibe* (a follower), and therefore a Muslim. Bay Fal women are even more submissive than the men. It is said that Cheikh Ahmadou Bamba became so gifted by God because his mother was the most submissive woman on earth. In their minds, women should follow their husband's will. If you do so, they believe, your husband will pray for you, and you will have everything you want, including successful children in life and paradise later. Bay Fal's practise what they call *'adiya'*, which involves giving your daughter or your son to a *khalife* or a *serigne* as a gift. The boys are used to work in the fields for the *serigne*, while women can either work in the fields or be 'kept' as wives.

In the third place, Islam is an integrating, community-building factor, certainly in a society where it is the dominant religion. Social events in which religion plays an important role are weddings, funerals, baptisms and, of course, religious celebrations. Women are involved in the celebrations by preparing food, organising the festivities, praying and paying social visits. The brotherhoods offer support to their members. The *serignes* give support to their followers, advise them, etc., and the members help each other. This explains the expansion of the Mouride in Europe and the USA. The interviewees mentioned the first, not the second element. The observance of religion earns Muslim women respect and a certain status in the community. To know how to pray, to be able to read the Koran and follow other religious observances makes these women earn respect as being 'virtuous' in their communities. This respect enables them to have more of a voice so that their opinions and ideas are more easily listened to. Islam also inspires them to organise themselves, to learn more about their religion and to improve their situation, for example in *tontines* (small cooperative banks) or other self-help organisations and even political organisations.

Interestingly, the interviewees were not interested in the doctrine of Islam. Theological discussion does not play a role in Muslim women's lives. In Mali, a public debate is going on between traditional Islam and what is called the 'Islam in Africa'. The latter group, Wahabiyya-Sunnis, accuse the other believers of not being faithful to the Koran and Sharia because their religious practice is mixed with pre-Islamic elements. A main characteristic of this reformist movement is its focus on the Islamic law, Sharia. The Islamists put emphasis on the dividing line between custom and religion. By juxtaposing 'correct' Islam to the life lived by ordinary Muslims, these reformists are making a break between tradition and faith.[26] Our interviewees do not participate in this debate. The Islamists, who in other places are very influential, are absent in the interviews. Only once a Malinese woman mentioned that her uncle was a strict Wahabiyya follower. For these women their faith is, above all, a practice. For them, religion means primarily three things, as we have seen: a ritual practice like praying; ethical norms guiding their behaviour which means respect for their husbands; and participating in the community and helping others, especially the poor.

Socialisation for these people is religious and takes place in the household. From family members, they have learned to pray by saying the ritual words and executing the ritual gestures and ablutions. Fathers are mentioned more than mothers, but also other relatives. None of the women interviewed had learned to read the Koran. However, this does not mean that there are no schools for religious education or that they are closed to girls. One of the surprising findings of the study is the widespread network of Koran schools to which the younger generation at least has had some access. In Mali and Senegal – especially in the urban areas – women attributed their knowledge of Islam to their attendance at Koran schools. In all sites, sending children to these schools to learn more about their religion was seen as a religious duty. Children are taught the religious observances. This means being able to say one's prayers by heart, since the children do not speak Arabic, and to learn the correct form of behaviour and dress, as well as other rituals associated with religious practice. Women who had been to Koran school could often not read the Koran nor interpret it. The women had lessons for only two to three years, while men were educated for a longer period. All these women say that boys and girls should have the same education in Koran school but, in practice, the boys' education is longer and more advanced. De facto, Muslim women are excluded from the religious field. It is very difficult for them to receive theological training.

The position of Muslims in Western Europe is quite different from those women who were interviewed. Because the overall culture of the countries in which they live is secularised, believers here are forced to think about what their faith implies. Everyday culture is not necessarily religious. They form a minority and are challenged all the time to justify their practice. For this reason they tend to assume a Muslim identity, although this can vary very much qua denomination: the strict Sunnis or the liberal Alevi. It can vary qua practice, e.g. strict followers of the obligations to occasional practitioners during the Ramadan; also qua ethnic origin: Surinamese immigrants from Pakistani or Javanese origin, Moroccans who are Arabic-speaking or Berbers. Turkish new comers: who can be Turks or Kurds. Muslims in the West are far from united and they look down even upon each other. What is the reason, then, that the West is so afraid of Islam? Is it because of a very small minority of Muslims who opt for violence, far from characteristic for this faith? Is it that a lifestyle inspired by faith is so far from their own practice? This fear reminds me of my own youth, when in the Netherlands the Catholics were perceived as potential traitors, the majority looked upon with mistrust – a fear that has long since disappeared,[27] however, not without struggle and a long process of emancipation.

In the relations between the majority and the newcomers in the Netherlands, politicians and media have increasingly pushed the last group into the position of the accused. Older immigrant men and women, sometimes illiterate, are now considered guilty of not wanting to adapt because they are not able to speak Dutch. In the interaction between the Dutch majority and the newcomers, the latter are blamed for the existing communication problems. The host culture is taken to be a self-evident 'given', and the immigrants must accommodate. Miscommunication is perceived as a problem where responsibility lies in the immigrants' groups, not in the host community or even in the interaction between both groups. The consequence of these attacks is the increasing number of so-called 'Muslim dresses', and the newcomers start to behave like the image in which they are perceived. The social problems are not caused by cultural differences but, among other reasons, by the low level of education of the first generation of newcomers. This has two consequences: high employment and a trend toward interpreting the Koran literally. In the meantime, the second generation of Muslims identifies with the 'Umma', the trans-national community of believers, and/or they participate in the everyday lives of the relatives and friends abroad via Internet and other means of communication.

Up until now we have analysed examples of diversity and differences related to everyday culture – the differences between everyday culture shaped by religion versus an everyday culture influenced by rational, scientific thinking and, further, the gap between a life of abundance and one of scarcity. The rest of this chapter focuses on some intercultural differences related to fields.

Hierarchy of fields   Young boys and girls employed as cashiers in Dutch supermarkets are trained today to greet the customer before checking the price of the products. Strictly speaking from an economic point of view, it is a waste of time, an unnecessary ritual. However, marketing experts are afraid that the image of the enterprise will suffer under a purely economic approach without any human touch. Seldom is there more human interaction than just an exchange of greetings. Most customers seem to like this kind of interaction, preferring this anonymous exchange to the talk of the small shopkeeper in the neighbourhood who knows everyone personally. In Africa the same ritual exists in the supermarkets, but there is no need to train the street-sellers in communication skills. Their strategy is already based on human relations. They always start their sales talk with human interest questions, such as those pertaining to where you come from, thereby looking for a common interest or experience and sometimes forcing the Western tourist, afraid of losing time, to speed up and get down to business. Expressions such as 'You are my friend' or 'I know you' are frequently used because they indicate a relationship. Hassling about the price is, for them, part of the fun of selling. And the first customer of the day's price is accepted even if it implies an economic loss, because this will bring good luck. And once the deal is closed, the seller has to give a small present because, in the end, it is not just a deal, but 'we are friends!' – two quite different ways of doing business.

Bourdieu would rightly see in this difference the gap between capitalist and pre-capitalist economies. But he warns us at the same time that those differences are difficult to understand. Analysing the concept field, we have seen how knowledge of the origin and the history of the field is indispensable for understanding its specific character. Economy has been very successful in transforming itself into a 'pure science', that is without a history and therefore capable of imposing its rules as universal and timeless. The basic premise of looking for profit has become part of common sense. It has become quite normal to openly express one's intentions to make a profit, to exploit others, and to accumulate. So it is very difficult not to perceive economy's laws as universal. However, today's economy as a science is the result of a large history of changing people's perceptions about exchanges. Even today, besides economy in the strict sense, other forms of economy in the broad sense of exchange exist, like in the household, in the religious enterprises or in the arts. In the Western household, not every activity is seen from the point of view of profit. On the contrary, profit is not mentioned; solidarity is supposed. Sex, for instance, is without a price – quite the opposite of sex as a trade outside the household.

In our societies, the capitalist economy has become not only the dominant model of economy but also the field that has been placed over all other fields. This means concretely that people tend to look at all human activities from an economic perspective. They tend to think in terms of the money value of the time spent in an activity, i.e. what's in it for me? This spirit penetrates all the other fields, colonising them and imposing the same way of thinking. In spite of the integration of economies in the capitalist global system, all commercial activities have still not been integrated everywhere. Take the handicraft market in Niger, for example. E. Davis did research on this market [28] and noticed big changes among producers and clients. The producers were generalists before, working for the Touareq nobility, now they are specialists working for Western development workers. In spite of those changes, the trade remains embedded in relations of friendship and 'clientele-ism'. Another example of pre-capitalist behaviour can be found in Samoa, where gifts play an important role in maintaining relations. Only money transfers from relatives living in Australia or New Zealand can maintain this system. A third situation can be found in the Muride fraternity from Senegal. This local Muslim organization, founded in colonial times, has developed into an internationally operating network combining obedience to a spiritual leader, a Marabou, combined with a labour ethic that finds them employed in Paris, Frankfurt and New York. From those cities, large amounts of money flow back to the holy centre of the brotherhood in Touba.

The coexistence of different economic systems can have consequences for communication. If the difference between a gift and a product is not perceived, then ceremonies such as that at the opening of the Festival of Pacific Arts in Noumea are senseless [29]. At that time, gifts were exchanged between the delegations of other islands and the traditional local chiefs of New Caledonia – among other things, yams and cloth with relatively low value. But the exchange is not based on the economic value; what matters is the building of relations. In such a traditional society, the difference between economic transactions and gifts can merge. The anthropologist Goddard who did research in a village on Papua Guinea best describes how confusing this can be. Upon his arrival, he received a gift from a person who he could not identify. The man made himself known again at the moment of departure, although no relationship between them had been established. The anthropologist tried to repair this by offering an extra gift, but both realized that it was too late. The same misunderstanding took place between the local correspondent of a Dutch paper in Kenya and his Samburu friend, when the first one asked to have a blanket returned that had been borrowed some time ago. What was for the first a loan was for the other a gift[30]. For the Samburu it is obvious that you share everything as long as available. They don't have closets or other ways to maintain exclusive property. Only very recently have people started to use boxes for storage that can be closed. Asking for a blanket back, while you have plenty of them, is denying the friendship. Alternative economic behaviour can be found not only among nomads or in rural areas, but also in African towns.

A well-known phenomenon is that of the tontines: self-help groups of mostly women who deposit small quantities of money regularly whereby each member can, in turn, use the collected money to buy something or to solve family problems. But solidarity goes further. In West African towns, life is characterised by extended networks of the exchange of gifts and presents – money, food, dresses, etc[31]. Small amounts of money and prepared food or fruits are exchanged continuously between people. Roth gives the example of a young man, mostly without money, who receives 100 CFA from his mother. Walking to his father's house he meets an old man, on his way to a funeral, who asks him for money. He gives all the money to the unknown man. This kind of gift giving is far from calculated, not 'do ut des', i.e. I give to you so you will give to me later. Indeed, it is not an economic act but a way of expressing one's belonging to a community. This further implies that you will not eat a fruit alone in the company of others. You will invite others to accept a part of the orange or a part of your bread. Luckily also in our societies, the exchange of gifts remains an eloquent form of communication; the difference is that we don't depend on these networks for our economic well-being and survival.

Development discourse and change Once we are aware of the alternative means of economic exchange between people, the failure of many projects in development cooperation can be explained. Again, two visions clash in this field. At the one hand the vision of governments, of the IMF and World Bank who consider human beings in their economic-ism as isolated, calculating individuals looking only after their own interests. At the other hand the world of real people who are not calculating in their own gains but are capable of doing something for others, preferring to be driven by their emotions, like solidarity and compassion, more than calculating reason only.

The field of development cooperation has known many fashions, from 'basic needs' to 'process approach', from 'institution building' to 'good governance'. In the long decades that international development has been active, always two main discourses could be distinguished. The dominant one is that of economic growth, mostly defended by big institutions and governments versus alternative visions conscious of power and interest and aiming at empowerment of oppressed and marginalised people. Since long ago the development workers have been aware of the dangers of blueprint thinking in imposing solutions.[32] Even the Bank has become aware of the need to organise participation of the so-called target groups. Many people have experimented with all kind of forms to integrate the farmers' ideas, wishes and knowledge in the proposed approaches to improve their situation. But the communication between experts and peasants, including poor women, is far from transparent or easy. In spite of all good will it remains difficult to avoid applying their own known concepts and categories legitimised by the sciences. Take the concepts of poverty or household as examples. We have seen already that poverty means different things in Latin America and Africa. In the West we tend to look at poverty from a rather economistic perspective and to forget the importance of the self-image of a person. Needs are created, too. NGO's give too much for free, creating dependency and ignoring the African culture of gift and counter-gift.[33] If he or she who gives denies the other the possibility of reciprocity, building relations becomes very difficult. Tony Vaux, who worked more than twenty years in relief aid for Oxfam (UK), analysed recently the motifs of the helping professionals.[34] Examining his own intervention during the civil war in Mozambique, he came to the tragic insight into the risks of power in the interaction with the poor:

'We are supposed to feel concern and pity, but sometimes the reaction to poverty is more like contempt. We have learned not to recognise these feelings; but that does not mean that they do not exist nor have an insidious effect, especially when we suddenly find ourselves in a position of power.'[35]

Organising relief aid is a position of power. The needy exaggerated their dependence, and relief workers did not see that food was available at the spot where people were starving. They had no power to buy it; food was channelled to the cities.

Gender relations and household are other areas of possible miscommunication. In the Western world, 'household' means a couple of persons working together to achieve welfare for the family. In most parts of Africa, a marriage does not necessarily lead to close cooperation between husband and wife. Each spouse feels more obliged to his/her kin from the father or mother's side. Solidarity with the lineage can all the time compete with the conjugal relations. Men and women perform different labour activities, but they can make different investments. Besides, a woman will never inherit land from her husband. It is even not uncommon for husband and wife to live in different places. And, of course, the relations in a polygamous family are more complex still. Without clear understanding of the local situation, both from a male and a female perspective, it is not possible to plan any intervention. Finally, the Western planning mentality – the wish to control everything excluding uncertainty – is another hindrance to understanding. If a foreign advisor, after he has expressed his sorrow on the sudden death of a colleague, for example, asks when we will depart today, he upsets his African team. Death is the ultimate denial of a planned life. Rendering the last honour to a person is infinitely more important than any work-related task.

In spite of the official rhetoric about partnership and equal responsibility, the communication between the partners in development interventions is mostly one-way communication instead of two-way. If only we were able to consider alternative solutions found in the South as an option for our societies, something would have changed. Our politicians complain about people's lack of interest in politics. Why not try to have a participative budget in which neighbourhoods and communities can decide about the yearly budget, like in Brazil and Bolivia? Why not use some of the effective approaches applied in the South to organise and mobilise our marginalised unemployed? Why are the possibilities for community-building given by the Islamic faith not used? Why not experiment with peer group information about Aids, as successfully tested in Tanzania? Finally, we can learn that a society regulated by a market consisting of calculating individualists is not the only way, nor the final option.

Conclusion: Limits to understanding We have seen that diversity is growing by the availability of consumer goods. People today have many possibilities to construct a specific identity and can even vary it according to the situation. People communicate via consumption patterns and lifestyles, e.g. the food they eat or the car they drive. Often this message is more eloquent than the words they speak. If we, along with Goffman, see communication as a dramatic presentation, then there is no doubt that today's consumption offers disguises, props, scenes and roles more than ever. However, to maintain the metaphor, the script of the play remains dominated by the progressive middle class – how to improve myself and my self-presentation. Person as a self-reflexive project is the underlying and common theme, although the script knows all kind of variations, like becoming happy, successful, famous, etc., 'thanks to my own efforts'. The story line is similar: the individual as an active participant in his or her dual role as informed and information-seeking consumer, and therefore citizen. In this sense, globalisation implies homogenisation. For the poor of this world, the constraints are so strong that their sense of place condemns them to accept their position as natural. Today's possibilities to consume increase diversity between people, but the real differences are between the rich – the cultural and economic elite and middle classes on the one hand – and the poor of the world on the other hand. This social distance is a cultural one too, and can be based also on the penetration by religion of everyday culture versus an everyday culture shaped by rationalistic, (pseudo)scientific ideas, like in Western Europe. Differences exist also between the majority of the world who live in the capitalist system and others who have not been completely integrated into the dominant economy. Those two are real cultural differences. I don't know to what extent those differences can be bridged. How does one bridge the social distance between Beckman as a football player and icon and African child soldiers playing with a ball to fight the memories of a cruel past? Maybe we have to accept that 'otherness' is a human reality that we should approach with respect, without the illusion of being able to understand it all the time.

Once we have mapped, next to national communities, other spaces of culture and cultural differences, it is time to discuss concretely how to increase our intercultural competence, our capacity to cope effectively with cultural differences. This is the topic of the next chapter.

Notes

1. Alan Bryman (2004) *The Disneyization of society*, London Sage.

2. Ritzer, George (1993) *The McDonaldization of society*, Thousand Oaks, Pine Forge Press.

3. Id.

4. Tim Edwards (1997). *Men in the mirror; men's fashion, masculinity and consumer society*. London, Cassell.

5. Bourdieu (1979) *La Distinction*. Paris, Ed. Minuit. Featherstone (1991) *Consumer culture & Postmodernism*. London, Sage.

6. Although the ethos of pleasure is typical for the progressive middle class, who set the trends, at the same time marketing experts discern an increasing number of post-materialists, who refuse to consume uncritically.

7. Helga Nowotny. Transgressive Competence; the narrative of expertise in: *European Journal of Social Theory* 3(1): 5-21 (2000).

8. Pierre Bourdieu (1986) *Distinction* (1986) pp. 365 e.f. London, Routledge.

9. Nancy Scheper-Hughes. *Death without weeping; the violence of everyday life in Brazil*. Berkeley, Los Angeles, Oxford University of California Press, 1993.

10. Geeske Hoogenboeze. Wonen in een verhaal dak en thuisloosheid as sociaal proces. Utrecht, de Graaff, 2003.

11. Rene van Bavel and Lucia Sell-Trujillo (2003) Understanding of Consumerism in Chile in: *Journal of Consumer culture*. V.3/3 pp. 343-362.

12. Van Bavel and Sell-Trujillo o.c. p.353.

13. Id. o.c. p. 354.

14. Id. o.c. p.355.

15. Emanuela Guano. Spectacles of modernity: trans-national imagination and local hegemonies in neo-liberal Buenos Aires in: *Cultural Anthropology* 17/2 181-209.

16. Inhabitants of Buenos Aires.

17. Guano o.c. p.194.

18. Lizzy van Leeuwen (1997) Air-*conditioned lifestyles; de nieuwe rijken in Jakarta* Amsterdam, Het Spinhuis.

19. Didier C. Gondola. Dream and drama; the search for elegance among Congolese youth. In: *African Studies Review* 42/1 (1999) pp 23-48.

20. Birgit Meyer ((2003) Commodities and the power of prayer: Pentecostalist attitudes towards consumption in contemporary Ghana. In: B. Meyer and P. Geschiere (eds.) *Globalization and Identity: dialectics of Flow and Closure*. Oxford, Blackwell.

21. Paul Willis (1990) *Commonculture* Buckingham. Open Univ. Press. p. 175

22. Canclini Nester Garcia. *Consumidores y ciudadanos:* conflitos multiculturales de la globalizacion. Mexico, Grialbo, 1995.

23. In chapter three we have seen that Tufte defends similar ideas on TV reception by poor women in Brazil.

24. o.c.145.

25. Nico Vink. Islam and the construction of identity of poor women in Western Africa. in: *Faces of poverty* Proceedings of the international CERES Summer school 2003 UvA- KIT. Maitrayee Muhopadhyay *Muslim women and Development* Synthesis report. Amsterdam, KIT, 2001.

26. Rosander, Eva Evers and David Westerlund (eds) (1997) *African Islam and Islam in Africa*. London, Hurst & Company.

27. See Olivier Roy. (2002) *L'Islam mondialise*. Du Seuil, Paris for a more objective vision on Islam in Europe.

28. Michael Goddard. Of cabbages and kin; the value of an analytical distinction between gifts and commodities in *Critique of Anthropology* 2: (2000) pp. 137-151.

29. Anthony Hooper (ed.) (2000) *Culture and sustainable Development in the Pacific*. Canberra, Asian Press. This book defends the thesis that culture plays a much more significant role in the local economies in Pacific countries than it does elsewhere.

30. Koert Lindijer (1995). *Een kraal in Nairobi*. Amsterdam, Prometheus.

31. Claudia Roth (1997) *La separation des sexes chez les Zara au Burkina Faso*. Paris, Haramtan, E. Kamden circulation monetaire et construction du lien social en milieu urbain Africain in: *Revue Tiers Monde* t.XLII n.168 2001 pp. 755- 772.

32. Martha Nussbaum and Amartya Sen (eds.) (1993)*The quality of life*. Oxford, Claredon Press, is the result of a conference on this topic that offers an overview of a long discussion. See also Nico Vink. (1999) *The challenge of institutional change*. Amsterdam, KIT Publishers.

33. One of the most hideous consequences of this approach is that most Africans who follow training, expect the so-called pro diem, cash for their presence.

34. Tony Vaux (2001) *The selfish Altruist; Relief work in famine and war*. London, Earthscan,

35. Id. p.95.

Chapter 6

HOW TO INCREASE INTERCULTURAL COMPETENCE

What competence? *Adaptation, integration? How far should I go? What are the limits?* This is the normal reaction of trainees in a pre-departure training, once they realise that life abroad demands adjustment to local ways of doing things. The question about the degree of adaptation to the local culture is justified, but not so easy to answer. It depends! I would say to somebody wanting to work for some years as a consultant or advisor abroad: adapt as far as you can and as much as is functional for the cooperation with the local organisation without hurting your own identity. In other words, in Rome do as the Romans do. It is different for sojourners who will stay in a different environment only for a short period, and different again for migrants wanting to make their life in a new environment. The Turkish president, visiting the Netherlands in the summer of 2004 in order to promote the integration of his country in the EU, invites his countrymen living in the Netherlands to integrate in the Dutch society by schooling themselves accordingly. Is what he suggests the same as what Dutch politicians demand from newcomers? Some of those politicians seem to be satisfied only with assimilation, expecting migrants to behave like the Dutch. The answer to the question of kind or degree of adaptation becomes more realistic when we again apply the distinction between everyday culture and cultural fields.

Expressions like integration, assimilation and adjustment have become programmatic objects of political struggle. However, once we accept, as defended in this book, the existence and the 'gravitation' in everyone's life of everyday culture, the idea of integration – and still more the assimilation of a person or group into the dominant culture during one person's or group's lifetime – is deceptive. More than that, it's unjust. A person can learn to speak a new language, maybe even without any accent, but the deep roots of the first socialisation of a person cannot be pulled out by force. Dutch missionaries who lived a whole life in a foreign environment and tried honestly, forced by their mission, to understand the local culture learned that, in spite of the fact that they often adapted as much as possible, they somehow remained outsiders and had to accept that they would never become real locals.[1] I conclude that we should not expect *adaptation* from expatriates going abroad, nor from newcomers living in the Netherlands; *adjustment* is good enough.

The literature about the adjustment process distinguishes, while using different names, an average of four stages involved when people move to another subculture:

1. *The honeymoon stage*: characterised by fascination and friendly but superficial relations with the locals.
2. *The crisis stage*: experience of differences in language and everyday behaviour leads to feelings of loss, rejection, frustration and anxiety.
3. *The recovery stage*: the crisis is gradually resolved as the expatriate starts to understand the language and customs of the host group.
4. *The adjustment stage*: the expatriate accepts the differences, and even learns to appreciate them. They become alternatives for behaviour.

According to the approach to culture used in this book, I will reserve the term adjustment and adjustment process for the local everyday culture. This does not imply that intercultural communication becomes irrelevant or even impossible. Interesting to see is how in the influential North American literature on training in intercultural adaptation, intercultural communication competence is a crucial issue.[2] Pity to see, however, how those texts remain rather abstract and unfocused; they do not explain what is concretely meant by intercultural communication. Why? Most of those studies are focused only on the individual level. In contrast, my book combines psychological and sociological approaches because communication, even at a personal and micro level, is complex and social. I will summarise the crucial elements.

In a meeting, the 'how', i.e. the process, matters as much as the 'what', i.e. the content. What matters even more than the so-called message are the relations which, constructed outside the immediate situation of the meeting, confirm or deny the identities of the partners in the conversation. To be recognised by others is essential for our self-esteem. Expressing this recognition verbally or non-verbally plays a crucial role in the communication. The same is true eventually for the opposite, for discrimination – the negative evaluation of a person. A dialogue involves more than the two individuals participating in it; the meaning of the interaction is finally determined by its context. In an intercultural dialogue, not only two persons meet, but also the groups they belong to. The supporters of both interlocutors influence the conversation; they look over their shoulders and even interact also. Efficient communication supposes scanning the position of the others, situating them in their social spaces, inside the relation patterns and even in the history of their group. Real communication demands that the special position of the other is understood and respected. And in analysing the social spaces that form the context of meetings, we make a distinction between everyday culture and cultural (trans-national) fields.

Intercultural communication competence. The aim of this chapter is to explain how our intercultural competence can be increased. What is meant here by intercultural competence? In the first chapter, following the normal approach of trainers, we have made a distinction between three basic elements: knowledge, attitude and skills. In the following chapter, each of these three elements will be discussed along with ways to improve them. Before doing so, it makes sense to explain what you can expect here and what not. It should be apparent by now that I do not offer a list of 'do's and don'ts'. Nothing is more practical than a good theory that, according to its Greek origin, means a view on reality. A new view on the world makes learning and change possible. Concretely, our program consists of the following four points:

1. *Insight*. I do not believe in the specific knowledge that endeavours to explain in advance what will happen in an intercultural context. Each personal meeting is unique because

unique persons are meeting in unique situations. In my experience, the most important elements for effective intercultural communication are two-fold: (a.) insight into the general process of communication as explained in chapter two and (b.) awareness of our own strong and weak points in the communication style we normally use.

2. The basic *attitude* needed for intercultural communication is openness for or curiosity in people who are different from us. This seems an open door, however this openness supposes a rupture with common sense; our immediate reflexes tend toward stereotyping people, and so we do not give them a chance to be known.

3. The central aspect of intercultural competence is *skills*, the capacity to perform. Most people have more social skills than they are aware of. The problem is that we use them often in a spontaneous and not reflexive way. As explained before, a basic capacity is to scan the social position of the interlocutor in relation to the other interlocutor and the context of both. It is also necessary to scan the development of the relationship between the persons who dialogue, concretely their concern with their autonomy and acceptation of influence on the one hand and, on the other, affection or being near versus distance or being different.

4. *Patience*. Learning to become more competent is a process of long duration. This is true for our first socialisation as well for the introduction to the cultural fields we are active in. A short training on coping with cultural differences can be helpful; it can function as an eye opener and motivate us to go on. But changing our cultural habits involves emotions; it is not just a result of a rational decision and, therefore, it takes time.

Self-knowledge   To check the preferred learning style of a group and also to confront them with the existence of different learning styles via a self-assessment exercise has been very useful in my trainings. I have generally used David Kolb's model of *learning styles*. Kolb showed that learning styles could be seen on a continuum or cycle from (a.) concrete experience: the involvement in a concrete experience, performing a task to (b.) reflective observation: stepping back from the task done and watching others or one's own experience in order to review what has been experienced, to (c.) abstract conceptualisation: a phase in which the events are interpreted and looked for the relationships between the facts and theories are used to explain the observed facts, to (d.) finally active experimentation: a phase in which decisions are made as to how to continue and what actions should be taken to refine the way the task is performed.

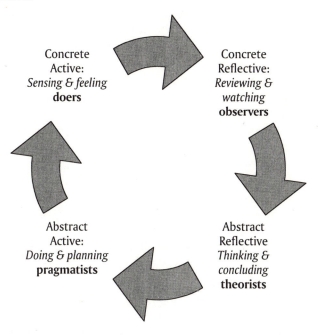

Concrete
Active:
Sensing & feeling
doers

Concrete
Reflective:
*Reviewing &
watching*
observers

Abstract
Active:
Doing & planning
pragmatists

Abstract
Reflective
*Thinking &
concluding*
theorists

Although Kolb saw these learning styles as a continuum that moves over time, in practice most people prefer and rely on one or two styles above the others. When organising a training program, the trainer should be aware of the preferences of the trainees because each style demands specific training methods: for the concrete experimenter, laboratories, observations, trigger films; for the reflective observer, the use of logs, journals, brainstorming and group work; for the abstract conceptualiser, lectures, models and analogies work well and, finally, for the active experimenter, simulations, case studies and homework are the most indicated methods.

Over the years, training approaches in intercultural communication have adapted Kolb's insights. They have changed from cognitive training about specific cultures toward an experimental approach directed at general insight into how culture works – from giving specific information about various aspects of a country, toward a type of training which puts emphasis on feeling and sensing as point of departure for the learning process through role playing and simulations, not related to any particular society.[3] This chapter cannot offer the concrete experience possible through training. However, I would advise the reader to consult the Internet, under Kolb's learning style, and do the assessment of your own learning style if you do not know what is your preferred one. Awareness of the preferred learning style makes it easier to decide how to improve one's own intercultural communication competence.[4]

Kolb's model is useful but limited in scope. Actually it applies mainly to the daily life knowledge as defined in chapter three. It applies to routine activities and talks more about improving performance and correcting errors, but is not able to explain how we can learn entirely new things. To understand that and to escape from the cycle of repetition of routine, we should listen to Chris Agyris and Donald Schon.[5] They have developed the concept of 'double loop learning'. Actually they did so in order to improve management's performance, but it can be useful for our case, too. They distinguish between simple learning, which means improving routine activities, and double loop or innovative learning. Simple learning is typical for everyday culture. Double loop learning occurs when errors are detected and corrected in ways that involve the modification of an organisation's underlying norms, policies and objectives. This kind of learning implies a rupture with the routine because it questions and changes the assumptions underlying the routine.[6] If we really want to improve our communication skills, we should, if still necessary, question our assumptions about communication, underlying our daily routine and breaking with that routine.

Another very useful tool for improving our self-knowledge is *asking for and receiving feedback*. Feedback is a way to let people know how effective they are in what they are trying to accomplish and/or how they affect others. Feedback offers us a reality check: is our self-image in accordance with what our environment thinks and feels about us? Trainers who organised specific training on it have mystified feedback somehow, however it is practiced all the time – certainly in education – informally by reinforcement of appropriate behaviour or formally by evaluations or examinations. In the Western world we have agreed upon some basic rules in relation to a specific form of personal feedback in organisations. To be specific and clear, focus on the behaviour of a person, not the person and behaviour that can be changed. Feedback should emphasise the positive aspects, be descriptive rather than evaluative, and be well timed. Be aware, however, that these rules do not apply everywhere. Some years of training health staff from Africa and Asia taught me that the rules of receiving and giving feedback accepted in the West need adaptation in dealing with people from those two continents. For example, giving feedback in public or to your superior is simply not done.

Feedback giving and receiving is not always explicit. In a meeting, the person who is listening gives verbal signs of response like 'yes' 'right', 'of course' or just 'umm', and also approving nods, looks and smiles – non-verbal signs of attention, interest, approval, encouragement and recognition.[7] Those reactions are conditions for an interaction that flows well. Interruption of those signs results in an interruption in the exchange. This implicit feedback has become second nature and mostly self-evident. Explicit feedback is different. Asking for feedback can be very effective, but it is not easy. In the personnel policy of most organisations is the performance review, an official management instrument that is seldom applied. Management and staff seem rather reluctant to give and receive feedback. Of course, feedback is risky because it can threaten our existential security. But even negative and angry feedback can teach us something, despite being painful.

Increasingly, other instruments have been developed in the last decades, like the method of *central qualities* developed by Daniel Ofman,[8] a Dutch consultant on organisational change. Point of departure for this approach is the existence in people of one or more central, dominant qualities. The central force of a person that colours his/her personality is: energy, courage, care, empathy, etc. Next to this central quality, a person happens to fall into a trap of the exaggeration of the main force. For example, a careful person can become interfering and an energetic person impatient. It is the shadow side of our qualities. Sometimes we are confronted with this trap when we receive negative feedback from an angry friend or partner. The trap is not the opposite of the central quality; that is the challenge. In order to avoid the trap we should develop the opposite of the central virtue. The energetic person should develop patience in order to keep in balance; the caring person should develop respect for another's autonomy. The fourth and last dimension of this model is the *allergy*, again an exaggeration, this time of the challenge. People are allergic to too much of it, e.g. the careful person becomes irritated by what by him or her is considered to be indifference. Flexible persons need to develop their challenge – the organisation of their work – but are irritated by rigidity. Ofman warns us that communication can be difficult, because what for you is a challenge can be your colleague's irritation.

Other similar methods can be found, but not all are equally helpful. At this moment the *enneagram* is very popular. This tool that you can find on the Internet identifies nine basic psychological types: the reformer, helper, achiever, individualist, investigator, loyalist, optimist, challenger, and peacemaker. Granted, nine types is a lot more than the traditional two or four, but I prefer models that can cope with the tremendous variety of real people without risk of stereotyping others or us.[9]

More specifically related to communication skills is our awareness about *self-presentation*. As we have learned, Goffman coined this expression in his 'dramaturgical approach' to communication. Interaction is viewed as a 'performance', shaped by environment and audience and constructed to provide others with 'impressions' that are consonant with the desired image of the actor. The process of establishing social identity is closely allied to the concept of the 'front', which is described as 'that part of the individual's performance which regularly functions in a general and fixed fashion to define the situation for those who observe the performance.'[10] The front acts as a vehicle of standardisation, allowing others to understand the individual on the basis of projected character traits. The front basically can be described by answering the following questions, related

respectively to social distance and our preoccupation with autonomy.

How do I mostly react to others' feelings? Do I offer help,
do I give compliments, do I give attention and respect, and am I
sensitive to others' needs? Do I smile? Do I use humour? Do I
show warmth and affection? How intensively and in what situations? Or do I maintain distance from others and is my behaviour intimidating? Am I cold and distant? Am I severe and fright-
ening or intimidating, and do I show macho behaviour? When
and with whom?

Do I project an image of autonomy by taking a different
point of view, demonstrating that you can be alone – an attitude
of 'take it or leave it', hiding the influence of others on my
behaviour? In what situation and with what frequency? Finally,
do I show myself as dependent by asking for help and provoking
feelings of guilt; by showing and exaggerating my own problems and suffering and expressing insecurity as to whether one
can cope? Again, when, in what situations, and how frequent?[11]
The answer to these questions can give us insight as to how we
tend to negotiate our identity in communication, finding a balance between near and distant from the interlocutor, and in
leading and following roles.

Social position   It is not enough to have insight into one's
psychological profile; understanding of one's own social position is needed to construct and maintain social relations. A
friend teaching at university starts his colleges each year by asking the students to design a map of the world, just a simple
sketch of the continents on an A4-page.[12] Especially in an intercultural group, the results are surprising: the form of the continents can vary enormously in size and form, but common is the
trend to design the continents in an ethnocentric way. Most
Dutch will exaggerate the size of their country; the Indonesians
will easily put Indonesia in the centre of the world, etc. Countries and regions absent in the map of some get a prominent
and detailed place in others. This illustrates how our common
sense understanding of social reality tends to be biased, in spite
of the normal sense of place most people possess. The solution
is not to turn everyone into a social scientist. There is no need
to be one in order to have a feeling about one's status in the

environment and the fields in which someone is active. We have discussed in chapter two how everyone possesses forms of capital or power in a different composition: economic, cultural, social and psychological, which determine our position objectively. Of course, this is not measured mathematically and the self-image of one's status and its perception by others can differ. This can easily happen with positions in new and emerging cultural fields.

But it is important to have insight into the limitations and biases that are consequences of our own social position. They can be consequences of one's class, gender, ethnic origin, or race. It is needed to replace the simplified perspective on social reality as the absolute truth, by a plurality of perspectives corresponding to a plurality of positions. Gender illustrates why and how. In the last decades, feminists have shown how the dominant view on reality is a male perspective, excluding women's views. Following in their steps, women and some men from the South showed how this dominant perspective was not only male, but also white and neo-colonial. In gender training, specific tools have been developed to make participants aware of the importance of differences between men and women, and their positions and interests. One simple but effective tool is to demand that the (male and female) participants reflect for a moment, and go back in their own life story to remember the first moment they realised they were different – a man versus a woman – and to ask themselves if the feelings evoked were positive or negative. The experience teaches that, for most women, this moment has been negative because it meant exclusion, for instance, from schooling while, at the same time, being expected to do chores (household tasks), while for most boys it was a moment of pride wherein they felt better, stronger or at least special.

In order to avoid simplification, let us consider some concrete cases. Some years ago a Dutch documentary maker followed three Dutch women who had each immigrated with her husband back to his native country of Senegal.[13] One of them was Janine who, in order to follow her husband, quit her job. In the film, she is irritated because the friends of her husband enter her house to watch television all the time. She considers this a violation of her privacy. Back home, her husband Tapha is happy and a different person:

'I am so popular. Everybody wants to talk with me.'

By emigrating, the position of both partners has changed radically. Janine has lost an important part of her autonomy and is not able to live according to the role of the most Senegalese women who live their own life in their own world. Tapha's status has increased enormously, from a marginalised black immigrant to a locally well-to-do and respected man. In vain, Janine tries to convince her husband to live according to the standards of a Dutch nuclear family. Finally she returns to the Netherlands. Perhaps a better insight into both their positions could have avoided such an unhappy ending.

Of course, differences in social position do not only play a role abroad. Take the case of Alice, a Dutch Christian women, living together with Rida, a Muslim born in Morocco.[14] Based on his religion, Rida objects strongly to the presence of alcohol and pork in their home. Alice has been educated in a family where every decision was discussed with all members of the family and everyone's arguments were taken seriously. She will not just accede to Rida, who interprets this reluctance as a lack of respect for him and his beliefs. His religious integrity is at stake.

Speelman, who brought in this case, sees this as an opportunity for negotiation between both partners and proposes several solutions like compromise, a redefinition of the problem by both or one of the partners, or agreement because she converts to Islam or because he knows to relativise the Islamic rules. All this is theoretically possible, but what is missing here is the link with the social environment, which limits individual choices. Rida seems to belong to the category of Muslims who takes the Sharia literally. How can he defend the presence of those *'haram'* goods to friends and relatives visiting his home? How can he betray his faith in a time that Muslims are under pressure in Dutch society? How can Alice abandon what she considers her rights in everyday culture and her autonomy, without betraying her own disposition, her relations with her family? Is love able to bypass all these problems?

Social distances are in most Latin American countries compara-tively a lot greater than in the Netherlands or Germany. For the Dutch working abroad, this can bring in conflicts. A young acad-emic woman who has worked in an NGO in Quito told of such a dilemma. One day a younger colleague arrived late and explained that she had a car accident. She had not seen the bus coming, and her new car was a total loss. She had not yet insured the car, but luckily she could blame the bus driver. Pity that the man lost his job and was arrested. The Dutch woman felt very angry with her colleague. How could she continue working with somebody with such a mentality? An aid worker in Nepal felt a similar embarrassment. A local colleague from a high caste refused to even give a cup of water to a lower caste women she was work-ing for; she put the water in the other's hand – afraid to touch 'an impure'. Both foreigners feel solidarity with the victims of abuse, but they belong to the same organisation as the 'abusers'. Causes of social distance are not broken down in a short period. In the meantime, expats should realize that they are to be per-ceived rightly as belonging to the rich ...the happy few.

Social distance between groups plays a role also in our own society. In spite of all possibilities to participate in con-sumption, subtle differences here in social and cultural capital remain visible and audible for the trained eye and ear. Our accent, way of dress, and use of etiquette betray us. Look at the Dutch accountants who have become members of boards of banks. They have not been recruited from traditional elite fami-lies, but are self-made men (and a few women) who have used the democratisation of university studies for an academic career. They are not necessarily trained, however, in behaving correctly at, among other things, a dinner. They forget to clean their mouth before drinking from their glass, etc.; they talk about wines according to a book but perhaps do not have 'real taste'. As a result, their employers feel obligated to send them to training.

In this vein, it is useful to ask ourselves the following ques-tions: How is my situation? Do I know the social codes because of my first socialisation at home? Am I very concerned about behaving in the right way because I feel insecure with people of a higher status? Or have I opted to be myself and do not see the problem at all? More in general: has my social position improved during my life or has it declined? Is the fact that I become older causing me to see the world in a negative light? The end of my life is not the end of the world, but does it feel so?

A training tool I have often used, because it confronted trainees well with their stereotypes and prejudices, is the simulation of *the bunker exercise.*[15] The group is asked to imagine that in a short time a huge rock will fall on earth, causing profound disturbance of life and threatening survival of mankind. The group of trainees is saved and can enter a bunker with resources for some months, but there is space for only six more people, so the group must decide from the 12 candidates who can enter the bunker and who should stay out. A short description of the candidates is given: age, gender, nationality, profession, sexual preference, education and characteristics like handicapped, blind, musical, etc. Explaining the reasons for their choices leads to heavy debates. In the final debriefing, I confront the trainees with more basic questions, if they did not already come across them, like: why make this choice and why not let everyone enter the bunker? Why should they stay out and you stay in? The simulation proved to be a perfect introduction to discussions about the official policy in relation to immigrants and asylum seekers.

Openness for and interest in others   Who has not experienced moments in which we had to recognise that first impressions of a person can deceive us? Consider, for example, the scenario of a girl who in the evening has just withdrawn money from a bank automat, is frightened by the sudden appearance of a boy with dark skin, and tries to walk fast away. The boy runs after her and stops her.... wanting to give her back her forgotten bankcard! What a misjudgement. Still, it is not difficult to understand the reaction of the girl: the newspapers warn us against assaults, it was dark, there were not many people around, and she has heard many 'stories'. Psychologists teach us that we are inclined to fall back, certainly in moments of fear and risk, on very old biological mechanisms that we have in common with other primates. However, in spite of the importance of the limbic system in our functioning, I would like to defend the need to control as much as possible our instincts and emotions – or better yet, to train them. Openness for others is impossible if we rely only on first impressions. Openness for and interest in others knows a passive aspect, avoiding stereotypes and prejudices, and an active one, curiosity about differences and respect for otherness.

The immediate, un-reflexive reaction to differences between people is often negative, varying from defence to sometimes abhorrence. Incertitude in relation to what is strange and unknown, or even abnormal, often evokes fright. The differences that cause most emotional reactions are related to everyday culture and common sense. This ethnocentrism, thinking from what is self-evident and seems natural, is human. It is caused on the one hand by the limitations of our processing of information, often without reflection as in the case of the girl mentioned before. Gudykunst points at the role of diffuse anxiety in dealing with strangers because of the unpredictability of their behaviour which would make the members of the in-group uncertain. But ethnocentrism is not only a psychological and individual characteristic; it is also a consequence of the way groups, nations and communities have been formed along human history via mechanisms of inclusion and exclusion. Today, under the influence of globalisation, those mechanisms are under pressure and have essentially become obsolete.

Ethnocentrism, stereotyping and prejudices are not the prerogative of majorities; those attitudes can be found also among minorities – all the more reason to take seriously those irritations about differences in behaviour and values. It is too simple to condemn such irritations as expressions of individual prejudices. Differences in everyday culture and behaviour can cause frictions, like smells of food in a common staircase, and what children are allowed and not allowed to do. Often it is not a question of bad faith, but of social images that are supported by groups. We have seen an obvious example of these mechanisms in chapter five in the interaction between caretakers and homeless people. We may generalise this example with what Gumperz calls 'minorisation' by gatekeepers – the institutional processes through which certain individuals are stereotyped as members of stigmatised minorities.[16] Gatekeepers are officials who have the power to decide about people's access to the nation and national services: police, immigration officers, and care officials. Gumperz made a study of selection interviews conducted in the British midlands involving non-native, English-speaking interviewees from South Asia. Members of minority groups tend to use communication strategies used in their original languages when integrating them in their English speech. Native English-speaking officials who, in turn, have difficulties following the non-native speakers' arguments react by falling back on stereotypical interpretations, like adopting a reduced and simplified English. Such behaviour should be controlled by training, self-observation and attempts to situate oneself in the place the other occupies in the social space.

How do we define the positive attitude supposed by effective intercultural communication? Using some key concepts: through interest in all kinds of people, respect for differences, the curiosity to know why people behave in other ways than we are socialized in, and a non-judgmental approach to people. Empathy is the key – the capacity to put ourselves in another's shoes. I hesitate to use the word 'tolerance' because, in Dutch practice, it appears to restrict us to a refined form of indifference – that of 'Let them be!' No, here we mean curiosity, mixed with respect, to see how others shape their lives and the world in somehow contrasting ways from the way we do. A word of warning against a rather risky opening question often used: 'Where do you come from?' In a poignant example, the Palestinian poet Fadwa Tuquan, who lived some time in Oxford, describes how she met a local painter who became a friend.[17]

'A gloomy weather. Isn't it? Our sky is always cloudy.
Where are you from? Spain?'
'No I am from…from Jordan.'
'Excuse me, Jordan you said? I don't understand.'
'I am from Jerusalem…'
'Ah, I know then. You are Jewish.'
As if he stabbed me with a knife…

It is obvious that the writer is hurt, even if she is uncertain how to present herself; or maybe just because of that uncertainty. If members of majorities ask the question of origin, it is mostly decoded not as real interest, but as a way to emphasise the difference between 'we and them'.

Tools to increase openness   In a race, all start positions are the same for every participant, like the distance to go. In contrast, the distance needed to improve our competence in intercultural communication can be different, depending on our first socialisation and the socialisation into specific fields we have undergone. Some of us inherited well-developed social skills from our parents, and others learned a lot by becoming professionals in specific fields more directed to human relations. In some fields more than others, social skills are required, like those for therapists, sociologists, psychologists, priests and politicians, although experience teaches that theoretical insight is not a guarantee of good practice.

What can help profoundly to open up a person's mind is a longer stay in an environment different from the place he or she has been socialised in. The obvious example is to *migrate* from one's own country to another, as in my own case from the Netherlands to Brazil. It helps a lot to understand the relativity of one's familiar environment. There are so many other ways to give form to your self-reproduction than that which you have learned in your education at home and in school. Such an experience can give you insight into the illusion of the self-evidence of everyday culture. The same is true, and again I can rely on my own experience, for the rupture that occurs when you change from certain professions in a later stage of your life. By this I mean leaving fields that have demanded a lot of commitment by participants to enter them, especially what are called the 'total institutions' or 'apparatus', like some political parties, or the RC Church with its demand of celibacy. I have experienced what it means to say farewell from a position in a field for which you have been prepared during long years, in my case from twelve-years-old on, and with a lot of effort and self-control. Recognising that you have to opt for a different future is not just a rational decision, it is a painful one, and can even affect you physically... but it also opens new horizons. Once you have gone through such a process, you know with body and soul that there is no absolute truth, nor only one way to look at reality. Granted, it is a hard way to open up one's mind. This kind of rupture from a certain position makes you free to assume new dispositions. Are there other possibilities? Could staying abroad for a shorter period be helpful? Yes, but not unconditional. Such a stay, especially when expatriates stick to the small and rather cynical world of other expats, can be very negative. Only when interaction with the local population has been part of the stay can it become a true learning experience, accepting another view on reality as an interesting alternative for everyday culture.

Could *tourism*, travelling to unfamiliar places, offer a way to open one's mind for cultural differences? Tourism can contribute to such openness, but only under certain conditions. Broadly, two kinds of tourists can be distinguished: those who look for entertainment and want distraction, and those who want to live new experiences. Among the second group – the so-called cultural tourist – you can find those who search for direct confrontation with different cultures. This way of tourism seems the best to enlarge one's horizons under the condition that they do not look for exotic 'authenticity'. The post-modern tourist knows that this does not exist. I had to recognise my own disillusion when visiting in the early eighties the local market in Kisumu, Kenya, where original handmade pottery was rejected in favour of imported plastic buckets. During the same visit I bought an original clay Massai girl's puppet with a 'dress' made of imported textile. Cultural exchange had been occurring already for a long time, and cultural goods are seldom purely local. New tourists know that they play a role in a sometimes invented décor with an invented past. They are aware that it does not make sense to look for customs from a past that has disappeared, creating distance between tourist and local population. Tourist and local population should interact on the feet of equality. You can find this kind of tourism in ecotourism in such places as Tanzania and Guatemala, where you can be the guest of local families. Also in New Zealand where the Maoris refuse to perform shows in the hotels, they now invite the tourists in their own setting where they determine the tone. In this way, the local people are not any longer reduced to a primitive and exotic alibi for a meeting with the 'natural' men, of which the tourist is not either.

Self-disclosure   An additional and rather obvious tool to openness is *self-disclosure*. It means 'individuals telling to others information about themselves that the other people do not know'. Self-disclosure is, at times, both important and hard.

Even expressing a positive feeling or a compliment is difficult for some people (see assertiveness). Why, then, is sharing our true selves with others so hard? Some families simply don't talk about personal feelings, so self-disclosure is for them a scary new way of interacting. Some people fear rejection or criticism; some fear intimacy; some are ashamed of their thoughts and feelings; some don't want to think about their own feelings or to change. Most of us have difficulties 'to break through the screen of stereotypes we are hiding behind' (Bourdieu). For most people, it is a great relief, almost an emotional necessity, to share feelings and daily happenings with friends, especially when feeling stressed. We need to talk. If we don't reveal ourselves, we won't get close to others – both in private relationships of everyday life as well as in the interaction in fields. Of course it is important to realise what we want to reveal to whom in what situation. This communication technique can be used not only between friends and relatives, but also with colleagues or even strangers, although in a different way ... trying to build trust first. A good illustration of how to use this tool in the last situation is given by Peter Griffiths, working as a consultant in Africa. [18]

'When I talk to someone on the project staff, I introduce myself as one of us. Like them, I work in the agricultural sector. Like them, I am not quite in the Ministry of Agriculture, and we can both feel superior about that. Like some of them, I work in the development aid business. Like some of them, I am an international consultant. This means that we can start talking in a private space, where we know the language, the culture, the problems. We are alike; we both know the background. 'If only they would understand.' The immediate result that they will talk freely about things in our common space..'

This statement may appear a little bit manipulative, but what this consultant describes is that self-disclosure is different in the spaces of everyday culture and in organisations in specific fields. But what matters in both situations is to identify a common space. Finally, other factors, like institutional rules, can play a role. By example, Gudykunst warns us that the use of this instrument is different in collectivistic and individualistic societies.[19]

Living with ambiguity   Another tool in learning to open ourselves up for differences is accepting ambiguity. An exercise I have used to illustrate this is *the nine dots* – relatively simple and maybe known to the reader ... if not you could try it. The assignment is to draw four straight lines linking all nine dots that are given in this setting, without repeating the same line twice:

What matters is not the solution of this problem, but to think about why it is so difficult to solve this problem. We project, according to the psychology of Gestalt, a non-existing square, which guides and limits our perception.[20] Culture works in the same way as this square; it frames our perception of reality. We should train ourselves to look further or even in the terms of De Bono, laterally – stepping outside our normal self-evident frames, irrespective if they come from everyday culture or from the cultural fields to which we are committed.[21] Depending on our learning style and taste, the masters of the world literature, like Shakespeare, Dostoevsky or film directors like Bergman, can help us in the same way, showing us mankind from unexpected and deeper angles.

Developing one's social skills   Because the position and disposition of people are linked, the ability to place the interaction with the interlocutor in the relevant context, (trans-cultural) field or everyday culture is indispensable. Following the suggestions in the field of Institutional Development, I will propose making an inventory of stakeholders, which means all those persons and institutions that are involved in the intervention. What does this mean in the practice of face-to-face communication? The following case takes place in Africa, but the tool can apply in any organisational situation.

Positioning   Some years ago I made a mission to West Africa to check the interest of the local museum toward cooperating in setting up an international system of art object identification and their training needs, all paid by the Dutch government. In order to determine their interest, a key figure to interview was the director of the national museum. When I introduced myself to the secretary of the director, I was offered a chair and had to wait. The director was '*malheureusement*' occupied. I waited almost an hour chatting with the secretary, building trust and expressing an interest in knowing about her opinion of the boss. Finally I was admitted to the office of the director who appeared to be in the company of someone on the staff. I got a few minutes to explain the purpose of my visit and ask him about their training needs. I told him how impressed I was by his collection of African art. In the meantime, it was lunchtime and the director did not have more time for me, indicating that I should come back another day. Walking back – the director did not offer me a lift into town – I reflected on this meeting. The director certainly did not look eager to cooperate. His behaviour was rather distant and cool. Why? His personality? His style of leadership …he behaved rather authoritarian with his staff? His mood that day? His ethnic background? Someone had informed me that his ethnic group is rather outspoken and proud. Was he testing me and the sincerity of the offer? Was he taking into account an anterior clash with one of my colleagues? Had he enough offers for cooperation and did not need ours? Some days later, the reception I received by a director in a neighbouring country was quite different – polite, warm and interested. However, once back in Amsterdam, the first meeting proved to be more effective. The superior of the second director, the Minister of Culture, was removed and the director could not decide anything, while the first proved to be willing to cooperate under *his* conditions. More important than the personality of the interlocutor, then, is the network he /she is part of. All those parties involved directly or indirectly can influence the outcome of a meeting. Of course, the situation and the genre of the meeting are important, but the context plays a crucial role.

In such a meeting, observation is very important, not only of your interlocutor, but of the scene itself. What is the layout of the office, where is it situated ... the centre or the periphery of the organisation, with one or two secretaries, a big or small office? Indicators of importance and power of staff members are the size of the office, the furniture, bookcases and books, the number of chairs, and also the windows. I discovered that the sponsor of a mission in Brussels was rather powerless when I asked her about her small and full office with only one window. She was the last survivor of her department, which was about to be eliminated. In another organisation, a foreign advisor to the director had been placed next to the director's assistant without direct access to the director! Not only the performance but also the scene of the performance communicates the actor's position.

Recently the departing British ambassador complained that Dutch society is difficult to understand for an outsider. He could not use a guide like *Who is Who*, where you can find an overview of the local elite, nor that you find in the papers memorial tributes to deceased persons.[22] His Excellency is right in his observation that social hierarchy in the Netherlands is difficult to understand, but what is interesting for us is his hint to look for written sources of information on local social hierarchy. They exist even in the Netherlands, although by other names.[23]

Scanning relationships   In the analysis of a meeting, we have seen in chapter two on tact and self-presentation that the concern with one's own face and that of the interlocutor play a crucial role. Let us illustrate this process with the story of Mathews Masayuki, an Anglo Nippon who, as a PhD student at Yale University, did research on the country of his ancestors.[24] He describes the first six months in Tokyo and his hilarious attempts to find his way and an acceptable role. One of the critical incidents revolved around a gift he received from a wealthy lady, Mrs. Tani, and her daughter Sanae. He had developed a close friendship with both while discussing the prospect of an American college education for Sanae. He had helped her with the applications and once everything was okay, they met again in an expensive bistro to celebrate the progress. At the moment of departure after the meal, Mrs. Tani handed the student a small, carefully wrapped box and a card; saying that 'it was nothing compared with all the help he had given'. Once home he discovered that it was not only a box of chocolates with a Valentine's Day card, but out of it fell five bills of 10.000 yen ($250). Mathews first reaction was anger. 'Who do the Tanis think they are? They can't buy me or my services!' But before giving back the money, he consulted some American colleagues and Japanese advisors. The difference in reaction was striking. While the Americans advised him to give the money back, the Japanese asked specific questions – about his relations with the Tanis and the character of the gift. According to the Japanese advisors, it was not a bribe because the gift was given after he had completed the favour to them. The gift, relatively small given their wealth, was a sign that the Tanis needed him in some way. He could not return the money because it would have been taken as a slap in the face. It fit into the mold that 'the Japanese believe that one has always to depend upon face-to-face relationships with specific individuals in order to survive in the world'. However, this was not the end. The student was afraid of becoming responsible for the girl once she was studying in the States, so he had to give back a return gift to set a limit to his obligations as receiver of this gift.

This case offers us an interesting clue as to how to learn to understand social positions and relations: don't trust your gut feelings, control your immediate reactions and instead consult local advisors. This is somebody who knows the subculture well and is willing and able to explain its rules to you – not necessarily a scholar or an intellectual, but an insider who is able to communicate with outsiders. How do you find them? Via existing networks.

Is this preoccupation with face and respect not typical for the 'Japanese' culture, and not in the West? Let us look at a situation quite similar: the case of the examination that disappeared.[25] The case is situated in a Dutch professional school where many children of newcomers are receiving professional training. The teacher lets a student alone in his office for just a moment. Once back, he notices immediately that one set of the answers on an examination has disappeared. Instead of four, there are only three sets on his desk. He knows that the student will deny it if he asks her if she has taken the sheets. He also knows from experience the fuss that will be made, if he asks her to open her briefcase. ('You don't have the right; you are discriminating!'). What does he do? He says: 'Ilknur, I gave you some minutes ago some pages with questions. I think you have put them by accident in your briefcase.' She looks at the teacher and gives the pages back. Why is this an effective strategy? Kaldenbach explains that the teacher does not impose his power, but shows respect for the autonomy of the pupil and gives her an escape without losing face. However, what determines the tension between both pupil and teacher are the positions of the teacher belonging to the local majority and the pupil who belongs to the minority.

How can we increase our skills in 'face work'? In my opinion it is relatively self-evident although not always easy; on the positive side, give compliments. Train yourself to praise a person everyday in your environment by saying something positive about his or her actions, and avoid talking about the less positive aspects that can always be found. After all, nobody is perfect! We all know that. Give praise: 'Very good, I liked your explanation or plan.' Say it, even if you have the feeling that you are exaggerating. In the same way, show consciously every day an extra preoccupation with others' front or faces. Avoid any possible loss of face by showing sensitivity to their feelings and self-respect.

Reflexivity versus spontaneity   Before going on, we have to deal with a possible irritation of the reader. Maybe you are thinking how to consciously give attention all the time to the relations with the interlocutor. Can you still talk spontaneously in that way? Well, we all need patience; reflexivity belongs to the learning process. Once it has become interiorised and a new routine, it will happen spontaneously. Lahire reminds us how children in primary school learn to assume a reflexive attitude to and a distant regard toward language and speech.[26] They are trained in scholastic techniques like grammar and spelling, focusing all the time on the form of speech. If children survive this, should we adults, not be capable of a reflexive attitude in relation to our own way of communicating? It is interesting to learn from youngsters from newcomer families. Saharso did research among boys and girls of those families with low status.[27] She describes friendships between those youngsters and how they cope with racism. Their strategy is not to smuggle off cultural differences, but on the contrary, to identify them. The boys do so by making the differences relative using humour; the girls show explicit interest in each other's customs. She found that class is an important intervening factor. Newcomers with low educational levels cope more easily with cultural differences than higher-educated people. Saharso quotes an Antillean youngster who gives his view on meetings with higher-class persons:

'They are a little bit too careful. They take their time, choosing their words, using expressions, like 'yes, relatively seen' and 'with nuances'.'

But such an approach is in his opinion not effective.

'Those people try to avoid that you feel discriminated or disadvantaged, but it is counter-productive. You think: I am not a child. Neither mentally retarded. ..Do normal with me, behave like a normal person, I like that more.'

In their daily interactions, the youngsters from ethnic minorities choose their friends with care. They look for people with similar experiences and similar ideas and they make a distinction between 'foreigners' and 'Dutch'. Not that they want to exclude Dutch-born youngsters, but they have to be open to a different lifestyle. They check each other's behaviour. What matters is that people give room to others ...or is the other a racist who discriminates? These youth have developed a skill to know with whom they are dealing. They have learned to scan by practicing it. Why should we not be able to learn it? We are helped by the insight that identity negotiating is not only a psychological issue, but also a social one. Politics and the media legitimise the social categories, before becoming common sense. So we should be careful in the use of names, labels and categories related to identities, focusing on persons instead.

Interpreting non-verbal communication   As we have seen before, we not only communicate through words but more non-verbally. How, then, can we learn to decode this type of communication? Definitively, the interpretation of gestures is not easy. As I am writing this chapter, the head of UNHCR, Ruud Lubbers, is under siege because he may have touched a female subordinate in an inappropriate manner. We know that Lubbers is also, by Dutch standards, a man who likes to touch others. On the other hand, it must be mentioned that the lady who complained about his behaviour is North American middle class. On a US-based Internet site, a consultant in communication writes about touching that 'it is often intimidating when the toucher is male and the toucher and touched are not close friends'. Being touched with such an idea in the back of your mind, you have to feel intimidation. For Latin American women, such an idea seems ridiculous. It is obvious that cultural differences play a big role in non-verbal communication. (It is obvious, too, that a man in the position of Lubbers should be aware of those differences.) Sometimes a distinction is made between high contact (Arab world, Latin America) and low contact cultures (USA, Northern Europe) Most of the studies on non-verbal communication are more descriptive in that they offer explanations. However, it remains possible to train ourselves to become more sensitive to this aspect of communication.

A rather well-known method is to look at the way our interlocutor is listening with body, legs and arms turned to me or turned away. That is the difference between interest and lack of it. Rather revealing are the non-congruent messages: when verbal and non-verbal messages are not synchronic, the person says, 'How nice to see you,' and steps back. Adepts of neuro-linguistic programming defend the idea of coordinating consciously your own body position with those of your interlocutor in order to influence them... following their movements, imitating gestures, even harmonising tone, rhythm and tempo of speech. However, the question remains if it is possible to consciously change our original body language and posture.

Frame switching   We have seen in chapter two the importance of code switching: changing from one language to another in function of the (perceived) relationship between the participants in a meeting. Here I will focus on *changing the perspective on reality* – from everyday culture to field, or vice versa, or between various fields. Let us have a look at some cases — first in the field of health, the subfield of leprosy care in Rio de Janeiro. An interesting situation that is paradigmatic for the possible plurality of perspectives on reality.

The situation of health care related to leprosy patients is so interesting because of the specific communication problems. In the sixties, Brazilian authorities had thought to finish the stigmatisation of those patients by officially changing the name of the disease to 'Hanseniase'. (The name reminds us of the Norwegian doctor who discovered the bacteria that cause the disease). Leprosy is, especially among the poor of Brazil, relatively frequent, although not directly related to poverty. (The incidence is four times higher than elsewhere.)[28] Lamentably, the change of name has only contributed to more confusion. Recent research indicates that the majority of the local population do not understand this name; some of them even decode it by still using elements of the old leprosy as causing deformation. Stigmatisation does seem to have diminished, but has not disappeared.

If we look at the actors active in this field, we have first the government health post, sometimes with staff specialised in leprosy detection. The treatment is free in Brazil. However, half of the medical staff does not even know that leprosy can be cured. Worse yet is the social distance existing between most of the staff, especially the doctors and the population. Secondly, in all neighbourhood pharmacies can be found all kind of remedies that can be bought without prescription – ideal for self-medication. Besides the official health staff and pharmacists, others are active in this field. Umbanda, a form of Afro-American possession cult, offers cures and, increasingly, the pastors of the neo-Pentecostal churches. They believe in curing people from evil by exorcism. In their sermons, leprosy is a biblical image of sin, which is often used. The population in the periphery can opt, when they look for a cure, between those professionals and self-medication. In practice, they combine the various approaches. The combination of health-seeking behaviour does not make a distinction between biomedical care and the forms of faith healing. The patients are not only looking for a cure but also for answers to the question: 'Why is this happening to me?' What is the meaning of it? Because of the different perspectives and interests, medical anthropology makes a distinction between the disease, the biomedical concept, and the illness the reaction of the patient has on the disease.[29] We understand now that it is not just a difference in individual perceptions, but a clash between cultural fields. For this reason, it is not enough that physicians are good listeners; they should look at leprosy through the eyes of the patient, asking themselves what this disease means for the patients and their environment. In East Nepal, for instance, leprosy is perceived as a curse of the gods, i.e. the patient must be guilty of a sinful act in a former life. It proves again how locality is an important aspect in this trans-national field.

This need for perspective shifting, which takes into consideration various and sometimes conflicting perspectives, is not only urgent in the case of leprosy. It is a more general problem. In medical training, effective communication with patients has become part of the curriculum almost everywhere.[30] However, the nature of the communication problems bypasses the skills of individual physicians. A recent study on the functioning of health care in southeast Burkina Faso looked into the reasons why the government facilities are under-utilised, in spite of high morbidity and mortality.[31] The research also applied Bourdieu's concept of field. It concluded that besides accessibility, cost and staff attitudes, we should recognise 'the importance of indigenous medical and spiritual knowledge as well as the impact of trust and social networks on the health-seeking process.' Local healers and a retired health engineer, acting as a doctor, have in this region a high status and are trusted, while the professionals in the service of the government are outsiders and perceived as such. Interventions aimed at improving the official medical services should consider their position in the field and not isolate them. In the case of Rio de Janeiro, seeing the fast-growing number of Pentecostal believers, the existing IEC-project should perhaps focus more on the pastors than on the medical professionals.[32] For the patients, the frontiers between the fields of health and religion are no impediment to switching from one to another. For the health workers, the opposite is true; they have been trained during long years to internalise the perspective of their field as the best if not the only one. Moreover, they have to face the competition of other fields, in this case the religious one. How do we solve this dilemma? Careful listening, even empathy, are not enough. Only conscious shifting from perspective, from the frame used in one's own field to another frame, can lead to understanding.

To finish this section, here's an open question for the reader to test your own skill in using different perspectives. Imagine the following situation: You work in an non-governmental organisation as an aid worker, in Maputo, Mozambique, where two computers have recently crashed under your hands. In the opinion of your local colleague, a medicine man should be consulted, because this is not normal anymore, but the influence of jealous people who want to get your job. The witch doctor can identify them and eventually stop them. What will you do ...pay for this consultation or not?

Dealing with limits to communication   In chapter five we have seen how, in spite of globalisation, there are gaps between the richer parts of this world and the poor majority, and equally between the believers and the secularists for whom faith does not play any role. Is it possible to overcome these gaps, or is it more realistic to accept those distances? Let us focus now on social distance caused by poverty.

Most people living abroad want to make local friends, especially when they are really interested in the host population. At the same time, people wishing to be friends regularly approach them and, invoking this friendship, they ask for financial help – a situation that is felt by many Dutch expatriates to be painful. What do you do, give cash or not? What is the relationship between friendship and money? How do you avoid being abused? How do you and I know that the stories told are true? Friendship everywhere in the world is ultimately based on trust. I have to be sure that I can believe what my friend is telling me. Sometimes people tell you impressive and tragic stories, which later prove to be lies, but that have motivated you to help them. Most of the ex-pats feel cheated in such situations. But why? Is truth really the criterion? Does it make a difference if the given money has been used for the friend's mother's funeral or the satisfaction of his immediate needs? Why do we want to know exactly all the details? Perhaps you have not been used, but at most your money or possessions!

Often possessions and money are the main reasons that make it difficult to become friends with the local population, even in societies where time for relationships is always made. Real friends ought to share everything. When the difference in resources between both partners is too great, it undermines friendship. We have seen in the previous chapter that aid workers also can be dominated by negative feelings toward the poor. I have to recognise that during my last stay in Burkina, I had this experience, too. By chance, I got to know some pleasant and interesting artists. In exchange for interesting and inside stories, I paid for their drinks and meals one evening and again the next. Suddenly I noticed that their friends shared our table and ordered food. Before leaving, I paid the bill and returned to my hotel. Later somebody from the company came to ask me if I was sure to have paid 'everything'. I understood what had happened but refused to pay for the friends of the friends. Now I feel ashamed for this stingy behaviour. I should have controlled my feelings of being abused. However, feelings are sometimes stronger than insight. And the social distance can be too big to be bridged.

Accepting one's own limitations   Traditionally, the Christian faith implied a consciousness to be a sinner, basically imperfect. In a secularised form it meant accepting human fault and failure, i.e. 'Nobody is perfect!' It seems that the new faith in the personality as a life project, the belief that each person should construct one's own identity, becomes a burden. It can put too much pressure on a person. Every trainer knows that each person can change only in his/her own tempo and at the right moment, according to one's potential. So we need to not only have patience with ourselves, but also generate self-acceptance, inclusively of our limitations. People need to be secure in their self-conceptions, have a positive self-image, yet not so secure that they do not feel a potential for change and growth. Development of intercultural communication skills demands equilibrium between self-assessment, belief in one's own potential and the awareness that each person can improve.

Dealing with differences is a complex activity and a real challenge to everybody's creativity. However, it can never remain an individual responsibility only. Coping with cultural differences finally is structured on a social and political level, and will be decided in the various cultural fields, including politics. The last chapter of this book will analyse how the Dutch society tries to cope with cultural differences and will suggest some solutions out of the actual stalemate.

Notes

1. Brother Maarten Bouw has worked during 40 years in Ghana: 'In Ghana they say that I feel intensely committed with them. However, you will never become a Ghanaian with the Ghanaians. You are and remain always a European'. In: *Berichten broeders FIC 34/4* p.18

2. See: . M.K.Asanti and W.B. Gudykunst eds.) (1989) *Handbook of international and intercultural communication eds.* London, Sage. More practical are: D.J. Kealy & D.R. Protheroe (1995) *Cross-cultural collaborations*; making North-South cooperation more effective. Ottawa, CIDA, and N. Vink (1999). The *challenge of Institutional change*. The last book is result of research on the role of international advisors on institutional development

3. M.C. Gertsen. Intercultural competence and expatriates in: *International Journal of Human Resource Management* 1/3 Dec. 1990 pp. 341 – 362.

4. Other differences made in learning styles are based upon the preference for the senses used: hearing, seeing or touching. The psychologist Howard Gardner goes even further in his theory of multiple intelligence combining the approach based on senses with approaches which distinguish between the logical/mathematical intelligence and interpersonal and even the intrapersonal intelligence. The positive side of this approach is the emphasis on the non-rational definition of intelligence.

5. Chris Agyris and Donald Schon (1974) *Theory and practice; increasing professional effectiveness*. S. Francisco, Jossey-Bass.

6. See BBC training and development on Internet

7. Pierre Bourdieu. e.a. (2000) The *weight of the world*. Cambridge, Polity Press,

8. Daniel Ofman (1995) *Bezieling en kwaliteit in het werk*. Den Haag, Servire.

9. The same can be said about the Belkin's model on the roles in teams

10. Erving Goffman (1969) *The presentation of self in everyday life*. London, Penguin, p.22.

11. *Psychologie* 15 Oct.1996.

12. Jaap van Ginneken (1996) *De schepping van de wereld in het nieuws*. Houten, Bohn Stafleu .

13. Puck de Leeuw. Grenzeloze liefde; made in Africa. Shown on Dutch television on 7/12/1998.

14. Ge Speelman. Interculturele communicatie als onderhandeling. in: *Tijdschrift voor genderstudies* 2004/1 pp30-43.

15. See: *Exercises for trainers* Tome 2

16. Gumperz. Interviewing in intercultural situations in P.Drew & J. Heritage (eds.) Talk at work interaction in institutional settings. Cambridge, Cambridge University Press 1992 pp302-327 quoted in Tamar Katriel in L. Wiseman ed. *Intercultural communication theory*. Thousand Oaks, Sage, 1995 pp274 a.f.

17. Quoted by Samar Attar: A discovery of self and other. Fadwa Tuquan's sojourn in England in the early sixties in: Arab Studies Quarterly 25/3 summer 2003 pp. 1-28

18. Peter Griffiths (2000)

19. W. Gudykunst (1998) *Bridging differences*. London, Sage. pp274-276.

20. More interesting is to expand this assignment by suggesting to link the 9 dots with one straight line. Several solutions are possible: fold the page with the dots in such a way that all dots coincide on the folding line; cut the nine dots and link them, perforating them with a pencil; make the line thick. Again the trick is to leave the obvious one dimension of the flat superficies and think three dimensionally.

21. Edward De Bono (1967) *The use of lateral thinking*. London, Jonathan Cape.

22. *Vrij Nederland* 19 June 2004

23. *Atlas van de macht* (1998) Papieren Tijger, s/p.

24. Matthews Masayuki Hamabata: Ethnographic boundaries: culture, class, and sexuality in Tokyo in: Card A. Bailey. *Guide to field research*. Thousand Oaks Pine Forge Press, 1996 pp121-139

25. Hans Kaldenbach. (2004) *Respect*. Amsterdam, Prometheus pp 39-40.

26. Bernard Lahire (1998) *L'homme pluriel*. Paris, Nathan.pp. 121-133.

27. Sawitri Saharso. *Jan en alleman; Etnische jeugd over ethnische identiteit, discriminatie en vriendschap*. Utrecht, Van Arkel, 1992.

28. 4 cases on 10,000 inhabitants.

29. A. Kleinman. *Patients and healers in the context of culture*. Berkeley/London, Univ. of Calif. Press, 1980

30. See for instance F. Abbot & RMcMahon *Teaching health-care workers; a practical guide*. London Oxford, Macmillan, 1993.

31. Helle Samuelsen. Therapeutic itineraries: The medical field in rural Burkina Faso. In: *Anthropology & Medicine* 11/1 April 2004 pp.27-47.

32. E. Post & L. Sansone (2002) Evaluation Projeto 2000; an IEC project for leprosy in Rio de Janeiro. Amsterdam, Nederlandse Leprastichting. See about the Pentecostal churches: Patricia Birman & M. Pereira Leite. O que aconteeu com o antigo maior pais catolico do mundo. in: L. Bethel. *Brasil, fardo do passado, promessa do futuro*. Rio, Civilizacao Brasileira, 2002 pp. 323-248.

Chapter 7

THE DUTCH DEALING WITH DIFFERENCES

The basic assumption of this book is that the need for intercultural communication has increased tremendously because of glocalisation: the homogenization of cultures which goes hand in hand with a renewed emphasis on local differences. In the introductory chapter of this book we have explained the theoretical framework of this study defining culture as a struggle for meaning. In the second chapter we have analysed and defined intercultural communication as dealing with differences in perception and evaluation of reality depending on the position of the parties involved. In the next two chapters we have seen what the causes are of differences. Chapter three explained the different way people has been socialised and how from there socialisation is giving shape to their personal reproduction in their everyday culture. Chapter four dealt with that other cause of differences: the existence of a multiplicity of cultural fields. We have looked at the limits of middle class understanding of differences in the fifth chapter. The last chapter gave an overview of the practical ways to improve our competence in intercultural communication.

Throughout this book I have defended the thesis that people's position in society and their dispositions are interrelated. An assumption we seem to share with the majority of people concerned with intercultural communication; however, for some of them the nation people belong to, determines their culture. Other approach intercultural communication from the perspective of the 'stranger', often perceived as member of a foreign nation. Taking the process of glocalisation seriously, we can not identify social space that determines culture, with only the nation state. Our continue preoccupation has been to examine what the possible other social spaces are, in which we are placed and positioned in, and what determine our disposition. We have analysed in chapter three the everyday culture and in chapter four cultural spaces and shown their importance as context of communication. In this final chapter we will answer two remaining important questions. First till what extent the concepts of the nation and national culture play still a role in intercultural communication, inclusively for the newcomers in West European nation states. We shall answer this question using the Dutch case. What could be a Dutch culture and how are the Dutch dealing with cultural differences. What implies the so praised Dutch tolerance? Ideal and reality are quite different. Finally, how to find a balance between differences and equality, could an cosmopolitan attitude offer an alternative for living apart together of the multiculturalism? Or is this an elitist illusion? First the importance of national culture.

What is the Dutch national culture?   Since September 1998 newcomers in the Netherlands are confronted with the integration act which officially aims to promote the independence of newcomers by offering them an integration programme under responsibility of the municipalities. This measure is not meant for everybody. The newcomers are required to apply for an integration inquiry, and according to the outcome of this examination, he or she will receive a training in the Dutch language and a social and vocational orientation. It has become policy that newcomers and recently also old-comers, who do not speak Dutch, should pay for this training. These measures have been taken by the Dutch government at the one hand to stop or at least to diminish the entrance of foreigners and at the other hand to stimulate them to integrate in the Dutch society. Public opinion and most political parties agree in the feeling that the Dutch way of life, the national culture is threatened, and urgently measures should be taken to defend it. The actual government under the direction of the Christian democrats have started a debate on values and norms with the same purpose

How to explain this collective preoccupation and even fear for others in a country known during centuries for its tolerance and openness? The outcome of the 2004 European elections and the constitutional referendum a year later made clear a deep euro-sepsis. Most Dutch will not accept to loose more autonomy to what is perceived as the Bureaucracy of Brussels. Another more important reason is the perception that the attainments of the welfare state are under threat. The immigrants and asylum seekers are blamed for it. The entrance of big numbers of persons who appeal at social security without having worked for it could diminish the solidarity which is needed to maintain the welfare state. But probably the neo-liberal ideas of the actual government are more detrimental for the solidarity because of the strong emphasis on each individual citizen to solve the own problems and the importance of the market as solution for all social problems.

National cultures   In many countries primary schools start the day by hoisting the flag and singing of the national hymn. Most Dutch don't feel at home when they by chance are present at those ceremonies. Big words like fatherland, people and countrymen are not commonly used in this country. Generally, Dutch feel superior to nationalist sentiments, with exception of the Olympic Games or championship in football. But nationality has become emotionally loaded. Benedict Anderson[1] has tried to explain why the idea of the nation has such an emotional resonance, not only during football championship, but especially during war in such a way that people are able to die in its defence. Nations appeal at feelings of community. Of course a nation is not a real community, it is impossible to know all its members personally or to enter in face-to-face contact. The nation is an 'imagined community and solidarity': the idea of a common link is an image. What is not the same as something imaginary. A nation is not the product of an imposed ideology or manipulation, but certainly is the product of a political project of nation building. Since 19th century a lot has been invested in European nations in a common educational system and in a national language. Both are objects of preoccupation of the State. Other institutions contributing to national consciousness are museum and national media. Reading a paper, like watching today the national TV-news, are rituals in which we communicate with the Nation in a common perception of reality.

In order to integrate the citizens in a strong and coherent nation state, politicians have always played the cards of what is common to all citizens and what is different. This was relatively easy in cases where the citizens spoke the same language and ethnicity coincided with nationality, like in The Netherlands. Other nations have been multicultural or multi-ethnic for a long time like USA, UK, India, Nigeria, Bosnia. In any case the national identity, the constructed common personality of the citizens, was used to contrast and emphasise the difference with the others, outsiders, foreigners and especially enemies. It is not easy to combine equality of each citizen for the law with differences between them. And many differences exist between them: gender, age, origin, economic and cultural capital. To maintain the social cohesion of a nation, inequality among the citizens has to be limited, if not symbolically straightened out. This is easier when state and nation coincide. National identity is especially crucial for the modern welfare state, because of the necessary solidarity between older and younger generations, between the weaker and stronger groups.

All West-European nations have developed a national identity in their own way. From the 19th century on the Netherlands have elaborated an interesting system to deal with social and cultural differences: the so called *zuilen system* or pillarization. The Dutch state has covered the present-day territory only since 1839 after Belgium's independence. From a cultural viewpoint the limitation of the Dutch territory was fairly arbitrary. The borders of the state did not coincide with the language borders or religious borders. Especially the religious diversity was to threaten the unity of the Dutch nation and its political stability. The education policy of the state, then in the hands of a liberal elite tried to introduce a general Christian education which should become the cultural basis for a national consensus as the Dutch Christian nation. However, the state did not succeed in reducing faith to a private matter. On the contrary, orthodox Protestant and Roman Catholics increasingly opposed each other and the political elite, in a political struggle known as the 'struggle for school'. The solution found to this religious group diversity was not to eliminate or marginalize it but to institutionalize it. In the 1917 Constitution it found its form in the principle of equal financing for public and confessional schools. Later a protestant and catholic university have been started financed by the State.

This principle of different pillars, recognized by the state became typical for the Dutch tolerance. Dutch society became divided into four dominant interest groups or blocs: Catholics, Liberals, protestants and socialist, which became the base of all organizational life inclusively political power. Both religious blocs incorporated sections of working and middle classes, whereas the other two were divided according to class lines (Liberals: middle and upper class, social democrats: working class). Politics became a question of bargaining and accommodating between the elites of every bloc or pillar. Most institutions were organised according the same lines: trade unions, media, voluntary organisations, social welfare. Everybody lived in the own pillar' organisations. Even marriages, friendships, jobs and other social relations were established inside the pillars. People lived apart and together: under the same State umbrella, but they rejected each others values and norms. At the same time the system implied in an emancipation of groups lagging behind. Oppositions between social classes were suppressed through the vertical form of organisation. Working class and middle class members joined the same religious organisations. The consequence has been that a middle class culture and lifestyle became dominant. All pillars liked order and authority and adhered to the same norms of decent behaviour. Explicit disciplining was not needed, it was rather difficult to break with the general bourgeois norm.

From the 1960s the cleavages began to erode. A growing secularisation of society, increasing welfare and of individual options, next to rejection of traditional authorities, made the Dutch pillar model obsolete. The dominant order came under attack. Norms and ideals of the new middle class we have characterized in chapter five penetrated all blocs. The concept of individual development became the dominant norm for all social groups. The meaning of tolerance changed again: it became tolerance as 'abstaining from judging others' (Kennedy[2]). Norms become very personal and individual matter. It is not done to condemn others or trying to correct them: leave me alone, and I will leave you alone. This explains among others why homosexuality has been accepted so early last century. It fitted in the tradition of giving space to the minorities and sexuality was seen as a private matter, something of the bedroom. In the nineties for the first time in century a government coalition of liberals and social-democrats made it possible to legitimizes changes in the moral order like gay marriage, euthanasia, abortion, and prostitution.

Since a few years the balance in the debate on norms and values has gone in the opposite direction. The Christian-democrat Prime Minister took the initiative for a debate and research on national norms and values. Again it appears how difficult it is to characterize the 'Dutch culture'. Foreigner visitors have often appointed at many characteristics, expressed even in English expressions like Dutch treat. The interesting aspect of those sometime mutually exclusive statements is that they tell us more about the speakers than about us Dutch. The books written by specialists to explain the mystery of Dutch national character seem to agree on some traits[3]. I will mention only two which are related: tolerance and egalitarianism. The last means the conviction that people are equal reflected in the classical Dutch saying *Doe maar gewoon dan doe je al gek genoeg*, act normally, that's mad enough. Meaning that original, outstanding or flamboyant behaviour is inherently unequal and offensive for others. The political and economic elites try to avoid conflicts and try to solve social problems by consensus; it so called 'polder model', exchanging information and to hammer out a workable compromise which all the participants can endorse.[4]

The overwhelming majority of the travel guide books on the Netherlands is not based on facts of figures, but on personal and subjective impressions. For that reason it is interesting to compare those statements with the outcomes of the official research by the National Scientific Government Council on values and norms. In a sub-study of this project, a longitudinal study on National norms in the Netherlands, van de Brink found like the main study that norms in the Netherlands are not in decay, on the contrary. The norms and expectations of the citizens have increased in the last decades. The problem is that they consider norms to be strictly a private matter and the citizens are not interested in the public maintenance of norms. Most Dutch demand for themselves the best, but when their co-citizens demand the same from them, they close the door. The data make van der Brink conclude also that a clear link exists between norms and social classes, measured especially by the level of education. A negative view on newcomers and emphasis on national identity was found more in the lowest social class (21 per cent of the population). He found also that (only?) 19 per cent of the Dutch is against egalitarianism, but in this percentage the higher social classes are over-represented.[5] Most norms are accepted by the majority of the population, especially those related to private life like household namely responsibilities, sex and gender roles. The exception are found among the immigrants with an Islamic background who adhere to more conservative view points in relation to family life. At the same time the researcher warns us not to exaggerate these differences. Also among the immigrants more modern ideas about sex and emancipation can be found.

We may conclude that the idea of a national Dutch culture is in crisis. The majority of the population adhere to common values and norms, but they are not interested in the public maintenance of these norms. What about the national norm of tolerance? How deal the Dutch with the newcomers in their society?

Dealing with new comers in The Netherlands   In spite of the common preoccupation with the raising number of immigrants the West European countries have dealt with them rather differently. Melotti summarizes the differences very well[6]. For the French the ideal integration is the assimilation: French like the French. In this process the school is given an important role. Deviant behaviour, contrary to the neutrality of the State, like using scarves can not be tolerated. In Germany the immigrants remain foreigners (Auslander), in spite of recent changes in the law. The big contingent of Turks are appreciated because of their contribution to the national economy, but finally they are expected to return. The British have again a different view. For them it is self evident that immigrants never will become English, or Scottish or Welsh, and that is OK as long as they don't harm the British way of life. And the Dutch, what is their way to deal with difference with the immigrants? It is important to distinguish, as we have done before, between the discourses related to the various fields, like politics, media and science, and the common sense of everyday culture! The first remain often rather abstract, talk about principles, norms and values, the second focuses on concrete cases and lived experiences. They have in common that in both domains the discussion has the last years hardened its tone. Understanding of minorities is perceived as 'politically correct' and thus suspect! The Dutch cultural fields involved in the newcomers situation are: the social sciences, government at national and local levels, welfare institutions. For the Dutch situation it is interesting to point at the mutual dependency between policy makers and social scientists. The people involved in those fields have often changed from State to science and vice versa!

Changing policy   It is impossible in the frame of this study to summarize the changes in the Dutch policy in relation to immigrants. Since 1974 an official policy has been executed in relation to those minorities, which share a common subordinated position. Minorities which are not in such a position are not implied in such a policy e.g. Mediterranean immigrants. Since 1981 Government policy aims not only at the improvement of the economic position of those groups, but takes also their cultural position into account. The basic idea is that all groups have the right to live according to their own culture, not only individually but also as a group. The tension that may exist between the norms and values of minorities and dominant majority is recognised, but is not dealt with. Easily, the rhetoric of the multicultural society is used, without reflecting really about its consequences. Sometimes the defenders of this policy appear to propose the the pillar system as a solution. Cultural minorities should live in their own organizations and institutions according their own value systems, e.g. Islamic schools; as long as the Dutch legal order and the underlying values and norms are respected. No doubt that representatives of the minorities have made use of the opportunities offered by the law. With an appeal on this principle of cultural autonomy, respect is demanded for norms and values which are different. Examples are female circumcision, defence of family honour in court, possession by a Winti spirit as reason for social welfare etc. The care takers of minorities have used this cultural argument in such a way demanding respect for cultural differences, that the public opinion has reacted finally with a claim for respect of Dutch national values!

Since the populist and openly homosexual Pim Fortuyn entered the political scene and mobilized large continents of voters, the idea of a multicultural society has almost been abandoned. The killing of a film maker by an Islamist extremist has even intensified this process. Respect for others' values and norms has changed into the political claim of almost assimilation. Immigrants should not only learn to speak Dutch, but behave as Dutch. In reality this change is not so radical as may appear. The official Dutch policy never has been very tolerant in relation to the minorities. A decade ago the sociologist John Rath has criticized seriously the official policy as 'minorization of minorities'[7]. Migrants are always presented as a social problem, as causes of social conflict and inequality. Dutch policy and academic research are in the opinion of this researcher at least partly responsible for the backward position of the immigrants. The newcomers are always defined as problematic. Minority and all other names used for the immigrants by policymakers imply that they are different, not adapted to the lifestyle of the majority and for that reason a problem. They also should 'act normally'! Up till now the Dutch government neither the majority of the political parties have refused to recognize that The Netherlands effectively have become a country of immigration like the other West European countries. In spite of the growing pressure by experts to recognize the facts of increasing immigration, the actual government maintains the fiction that it would be possible to expel the so called illegal.

It would be too easy to blame only the state for this blind spots. Ii is interesting to look at a specific case: the intention of the secretary of state van der Ploeg, responsible for the governmental policy related to the arts to change this policy in favour of the minorities. His very straight forward policy document called *Space for cultural diversity* (1999) started with the statement that the subsidized art sector appeared to be a monoculture which excludes the not-indigenous part of the Dutch population! The culture of the minority disappears in the culture of the majority. Subsidized art is facilitating only the access of the higher and upper middle classes to cultural events. The document proposes to consider culture as a confrontation: it should teach people to accept to live with differences. Culture is defined as a common arena of struggle. The document gives some concrete suggestions like that the museums should revise their collections taking into account the interests of immigrants and that the scenic arts should program taking into account not only the taste but also the possibilities of the immigrants e.g. programming at Sunday afternoon making it possible for the girls to participate. The financial consequences of this policy chance are very reduced. However the reaction of the Dutch cultural establishment has been devastating. They expressed clearly the fear of the elite that their self-evident privileges were put in doubt. No wonder that when now more than five years have passed since that initiative, nothing has structurally changed in favour of the minorities. The Dutch cultural elite has proved to be able to defend its interests. Luckily especially writers descending from the immigrant population proofed to find their way in the field of Dutch literature and have become accepted, first only as exotic, but increasingly as belonging to the field.

Another illustrative point of exchange between Dutch public fields, like politics, and the religious field of Islam is about homosexuality. From time to time Dutch media 'discover' that Islam is opposed against the open practice of homosexuality and immediately starts a heathen discussion with the apparent aim to show how this religion is traditional, even backward. A well known incident has been a sermon of an Imam active in a Rotterdam mosque and quoted and later interviewed on TV. More recently the media discovered that a traditional pamphlet was sold in a mosque in Amsterdam inviting 'to throw homosexuals down from high buildings'. Of course, even if believers appeal on the Koran as Gods word to condemn homosexuality, there is no reason to do that in way which is offensive for this minority, calling them sick or worse than pigs or dogs. What is rather curious is the way these discussions are taking place. They take the form of the good guys versus the bad guys. The progressive, open and tolerant Dutch nationals against the traditional, fanatic Muslims. Of course the reality is more complex. The Koran is not the only holy book which seems to condemn homosexuality. It took a lot of Christians time to learn to reinterpret the bible. And read those books in their historical context. Belief and practice are quite different. Homosexuality is practiced among the Muslim immigrants, like in their countries of origin. A very personal book tells us of the problems young

Muslims experience to reconcile their faith with their personal feelings.

I don't dare to be who I am, but Allah has wanted that way. The
Koran prohibits homosexuality. I don t want to disappoint Allah,
so I hide my feelings. Maybe I will become crazy, but I hope it will
not be that bad[8].

Such self-denial can be dramatic. But the Dutch majority forgets that only ten years ago the Christian-democrats had still opposed the gay marriage in parliament. The majority forgets too that their way to deal with homosexuality, like most differences, is to consider it a private matter. Sexuality is in The Netherlands mostly discussed from a dominant self evident male heterosexual point of view without the openness to put that in question. Tolerance as an empty concept what means in practice indifference[9].

Cultural differences are not only discussed in cultural fields or object of policies, it is at stake in a concrete way in the everyday culture of people especially in the public space of the urban neighbourhoods.

Everyday culture in the urban neighbourhoods of big cities   The non-western immigrants have established themselves for all in the traditional working class neighbourhoods of the four big cities: Amsterdam, Rotterdam Den Hague and Utrecht. They represent in average less than 10 per cent of the Dutch population, in those neighbourhoods their number is near half or even more of the total population[10]. For that reason those neighbourhoods are the right places to check how integration process is occurring in everyday culture. Since the 60s the population of those neighbourhoods has drastically changed[11]. originally their population consisted of extended working class families, whose members had been born there and remained their whole life. Many working class families have used the opportunity offered to them by increased salaries and urban renovation, to move to new build neighbourhoods or new planned cities. The old and rather small houses have been occupied by newcomers: students and one person households and immigrants living first in pensions but later with their families in those cheaper houses. In the meantime the originally working class population does not longer want to move and lives together with the two other categories sharing the same public space.

Each of those groups wants to live their own life also in the public spaces. Those lifestyles are as different as their everyday cultures. It is not easy to find an equilibrium between being near each other in those public spaces like street or common portals, and maintaining a certain distance avoiding to invade each others privacy. It is obvious that this public space has become an arena for struggle. The traditional residents can not longer impose their unwritten rules; and the other categories live now long enough there to consider themselves with the right to set their own norms in public space. It cost the original residents a lot to accept this change of norms. Verkuyten did research among a working class group in a traditional neighbourhood in Rotterdam[12]. He found that the informal rules of social intercourse are self-evident for the traditional residents. They are very irritated by the trespassing of these rules by what they call 'the foreigners'. Not only things like cleaning the portal, the loudness of the music, parking the car but also ways of addressing and speaking. Refusal or even incapacity of speaking Dutch and using other languages in public spaces is a source of irritation. One of the interviewees told how she tried to censor the use of Turkish by the employees of a shop in the neighbourhood. She discussed it with the chief, wrote a letter of complaint to the direction:

I am in the Netherlands. I buy in a Dutch shop, let them talk
Dutch with each other. It is not nice either if a Turk would be
alone among Dutch without understanding them. You will think
that they talk about you.[13]

Other points of friction are the education and control of the children.

Interesting is to understand how the original residents explain the differences they experience with the newcomers. Differences in behaviour between original population and immigrants are explained as consequence of their culture. The new comers are perceived as the opposite of ' we workers' and the gap between both groups as unbridgeable. The ways this explanation is used can vary, but always the victims of social inferior positions are declared guilty. Their awkward position is explained by the differences in values and norms, especially religious, not by discrimination, social class or racism. Look for instance at the way those Dutch talk about increasing indices of criminality in their neighbourhood. To quote a typical statement:

I say that it is because of the younger generation of foreigners, unemployment. Those kids live in two cultures. The parents have a culture which originates from ten years before the war, I think, from Morocco and Turkey. Those kids have been born here and watch a quite different behaviour of the Dutch children; they want that too. Their parents do not accept that. So friction arises. Those kids start to quarrel with their parents, leave their homes, and where do they end? Exactly in such a criminal world, isn't it?...[14]

In this statement the parents culture is held responsible for the annoyance the neighbourhood experiences by the deviant behaviour of immigrant youngsters. It is a clear example of a discourse based upon a opposition between we and them, in which elements of an outdated anthropology are used, to explain differences as a cultural problem only.

It is striking to notice in those interviews how people try hard to avoid the traditional racism. Also in these neighbourhoods the traditional racism has become old fashioned, but at the same time cultural racism becomes more influential. This does not imply that racism has disappeared. Listen to a black policeman born in Surinam and working in Amsterdam, considered to be a tolerant town:

Dealing with my colleagues is most difficult, white colleagues.. Yes, eight hours a day, as you work there, they remind you that you are black. It can be Ben Johnson using dope, – I see damn what is the link with me, he lives in Canada – or Neli Coman failing to run the 60 metres, or an Ajax football player kicking somebody down, you can not imagine the reproaches.[15] The white colleagues of this policeman will not consider this as racism, for them it is just a joke, which he should be able to cope with. Remains the fact that it is an example of what Essed has baptized 'everyday racism'[16]

In spite of the common sense cultural racism by the original residents of these neighbourhoods, they point at a real communication problem; different everyday cultures clash here. Let us have a look at daily life from the perspective of the immigrants. Ruben Gowricharn, self born in Surinam, can guide us. He wrote a nice essay on frictions in public space starting with a concrete example. A group young creole enters a tram-wagon and is 'occupying' this space. Their behaviour is noisy, shouting, laughing, and commenting everything. They talk in a mixture of Dutch and Papiamento. Often they have a tuner with them which is not listened, but audible in every corner of the tram. The cold faces of the rest of the passengers show that something is wrong. Their norms are violated like you should speak Dutch when others are present, you do not behave in public space like at home. A kind of behaviour that can be shown by other ethnic groups like Moroccans and also 'white ' boys. Also between generations the norms about how to behave are different. This kind of situation everybody knows from own experience, inclusively the feelings that are caused by it. More interesting is Cowricharn's explanation.

He sees an historical link with the former pillarization of Dutch society. This, we saw it before, was characterized by uniformity of behaviour in the in-group of the own pillar, while the differences with other pillars, the out-groups, was emphasized. The families living inside the own pillar were free to despise the outsiders of other pillars, but sometimes it was necessary to meet people outside the own pillar. According to Cowricharn [17] the solution found was the separation between private and public space. The last was considered neutral and open for everybody as long as people behaved not like at home. This model is not only bypassed by the disappearance of the pillars is the argument, but it is impossible in itself. The public space has never been neutral neither open for everybody's preference. The dominant group, the bourgeoisie has always imposed its norms. If we look at the difference between homosexuals and heterosexuals we find another argument for this thesis. People are allowed to behave as homosexual in the private sphere, at home preferently in the dormitory, but do not bother the heterosexual majority.

The model of private versus public space does not function either because of the different worlds are no any longer closed, but mixing with each other. Every group brings the own everyday culture in. Cowricharn continues: Irritations and frictions in public spaces are quite normal; we should accept that. But according to our guide, we Dutch are not capable to cope with differences, and clashes of values: 'They want to pacify or in plain Dutch: 'de verschillen plat slaan' (squeese the differences flat)[18] The mentioned polder model suggest this preoccupation with conflict avoiding, but Gowricharn's statement is too general and a stereotype. Probably it is true for the middle class but Dutch working class is able to assume confrontations and fight as they do in everyday life. However, we also should avoid unilateral cultural explanations. Let us look at the social position of the newcomers.

Social position of the immigrants   Disposition and social position are interrelated. We can make only valid statements on the integration of the newcomers if we look at their social position in the Dutch society. It is impossible to generalize; there are big differences between western and non-western immigrants; between Muslims and non-Muslims. In the framework of this study is impossible even to summarize all the recent studies on the position of the newcomers. I limit myself to some important points:

- To describe and explain the position of newcomers and their children, often the common sense image of a generation in between cultures is used. An image which is misleading. Cultures are not outside people, they mix all the time. Newcomers in order to survive make a lot of the rules existing in the new environment their own. Especially the young second generation is actively learning and adjusting. We have seen that the second generation is skilled in code switching which in stead of an offence of the Dutch should be seen as an asset.[19]
- Among the specialists in immigration studies the concept of transnational communities has become popular.[20] Thomas Faist warned that transnational space is not necessarily formed by transnational communities also by kinship groups and trans-

national circuits. Transnational social spaces are combinations of ties, positions in networks and organisations, and networks of organisations that reach across the borders of multiple states. The links with the country of origin can be informal like family tie or formal, institutionalized such as political parties entertaining branches in various countries. Which intervening factors decide the strategies of migrants/ refugees? The first studies on the Dutch situation have been published.[21] They show a great variety in strategies and positions, but also that transnational links not necessarily should form a hindrance for adjustment.

- The traditional Islamic concept of society supposes to live in Muslim society; the theologians have not elaborated principles for Muslims living as minorities in secular states.[22] In the meantime the second generation of Turks and Moroccans identifies themselves strongly with a Muslim identity. Without practicing the rules of the faith strictly, this identification helps them to find their way in the Dutch society.[23] Minority groups are not collective actors; they are divided in factions and subgroups.

Taking into account the specific and often difficult social position of the newcomers will prevent us to understand social frictions between minorities and majority as a consequence of a shock between national cultures like 'Dutch culture' versus 'the Moroccan culture', or equally superficial between modernity and tradition.

Between us and them   The short overview which we gave of the interaction in fields and everyday life between original Dutch and the newcomers permits us to conclude that the Dutch up till now did not find a balance between equality and difference. What to do? According to Verkuyten there are basically two strategies to be used: 1. Recognizing and respecting the differences between people or 2. To find an umbrella identity which can unite the different groups in a new united we that bypasses the differences. Although the tone of the Dutch debate about dealing with differences is too harsh, it offers opportunities to take the existing cultural differences seriously and so, thanks to intercultural communication, to construct mutual understanding.

Dealing with differences: gender as example Gender studies and the international women movement have in their own way made clear the tension between equality and differences, in this case between men and women. That both gender have the same values is recognised now in the Western world, at least in theory, at the same time that the differences are recognized. A lot of studies have been published about the renewed vision on gender relations. Giddens puts a lot of emphasis on the transformation of intimacy; new forms of relations and love.[24] His optimistic thesis is that the new forms of relationships offer unknown possibilities for personal and social emancipation. In his view the traditional ideal of romantic love, is replaced by a new form, the confluent love, 'active, contingent love and therefore jars with 'forever', 'one and only' qualities of romantic love complex. What holds the relationship together, is the acceptance on the part of each partner that each of them gains sufficient benefit from the relation to make it worthwhile. If one of the partners does not see any advantage in the relationship, it is finished. The separation between sexuality and reproduction makes more equality possible between the partners. The new 'plastic' sexuality can assume many forms and makes the relationship more free. Also in the intimate sphere we can find a plurality of identities. Relationships, friendships and sexual relationships are not fixed for ever, but demand continuous effort to give them form. In spite of his optimism Giddens recognizes the risks of these developments. One of them is the open character of what is possible between the sexes. Role patterns have become confused, especially for men; another risk is the position of children.

Is it possible to escape from our gender identity? For sure gender is strongly influenced by culture and history, but at the same time biologically grounded. You are man or woman, is not? The influential feminist Judith Butler defends in her books the opposite view[25]. You *are* not a man or woman, but you *are made* male or female through repetition of gestures and positions. Each of us has repeated these practices so many times that they appear to be natural. (They have been interiorized, they are part of our body language). But travesties, cross-dressing and the lesbian butch femme creations prove in Butler's view that sexual identities are not fixed. In these practices men can assume female identities and vice versa. Differences are not natural but constructed. Butler is not the only one who prefers to talk about queer identities in stead of a particular form of sexual identity. Queer represents any number of positions arrayed in opposition to oppressive social and cultural norms and policies related to sexuality and gender. In the early 90ties the 'Queer Nation' became the movement which reunited all sexual minorities in defence of their rights. Already after some years this movement has collapsed under the tension between diversity of the various identities and the sameness of all members symbolised by the Nation.

The failure of the Queer nation movement does not deny the utopian character of the gender identities as practiced in gay and lesbian movement. The political avant-garde of this movement has always resisted to accept the dominant heterosexual form of sexuality. The principles are the male sexual active role, penetration and the female passivity, being penetrated. Or expressed more plastically like in the Brazilian popular language: eating or being eaten, each role implying in inequality and difference in status. Gays can of course fall back in the traditional division of roles in which dominance is crucial. They can also give their relationships an alternative form in which equality between the partners is more important. Gay prove so that sexual relationships not necessarily have to be based upon inequality in power as in the traditional heterosexual relationship. This is according to Bourdieu[26] a symbolic rupture with the dominant model. The principles that produce both stigmatization and the stigmatized groups are overcome. This new alternative sexual practice shows society that cultural differences and equality can go together.

The praise of gay utopia does not imply in an unconditional support for what is called identity politics, adopted by various minorities in the USA, blacks, women, gays; and later elsewhere copied as a model for emancipation, inclusively in the Netherlands. The risk of this approach is to reduce an individual to a group identity, denying that a person's identity can change and that most of us are characterized by a multiplicity of identities. Group pressure should never diminish individual freedom, prohibiting a change of identity. It makes no difference if this change is from hetero to queer, from Muslim or Christian to agnostic, from Dutch to American or vice versa.

Differences between people, real or supposed, can be and are used to stigmatize them. It would be already a great step forwards if categories, names and labels are not any longer used to subordinate others. Differences should be respected and not abused. The imam who according to his literal interpretation of the Koran, condemns homosexuality, has in a democratic society the right to do so, as long as he respects people who practice this sexual preference as human beings. He has the same right to be respected and not to be labelled for instance as backwards, as long as he follows his religious conviction, respecting others in their differences. However, from everybody living in a post-modern society can be demanded a capacity of frame switching, to be able to look at reality from the perspective of the other, inclusively from a pastor and/or an imam. (Compare chapter 6).

Cosmopolitan identity   If we look for un umbrella identity which could unite in the Netherlands rather different people, the second possible strategy, we can discard Dutch national culture or nationalism. The first part of this chapter has shown its limitations and contradictions. Europe maybe? In a recent article[27] Ash Amin defends the idea of Europe that could bind cultural pluralism and differences; an Europe not based upon a myth of origin, no myth of destination, only the commitment to a democratic space with rights not only for citizens but for all residents. A nice ideal, but with the increasing euro-sepsis everywhere in Europe difficult to realize.[28]

Could cosmopolitanism offer this umbrella identity? One of the first to link globalisation and cosmopolitan attitude has been Ulf Hannerz.[29] He defined it as a state of mind open to other cultures and differences. Elaborating this definition, he opposed cosmopolitans and locals. The last category are people whose cultural perspectives always remains below the horizon of their particular locality; cosmopolitans on the contrary are people on the move, wanting to immerse themselves in divergent cultural experiences. The spiritual mobility of the cosmopolitan is not the same as travelling worldwide. Not all travellers are cosmopolitans, most are not. However, the opposition between cosmopolitans and locals tends to denigrate the latter as narrow minded and conservative. John Tomlinson is right when he criticizes this approach as rather elitist.[30] Why should interest in and attachment to locality be considered to be of lower value? What right a cultural elite has to rise above the petty concerns of the everyday? In Tomlinson's opinion: the cosmopolitan disposition does not have to exclude the perspective of the local; I think it is more: the exclusion of the local perspective is impossible, because human beings are embodied and always locally situated. Of course it is possible to live somewhere without any preoccupation with the place. For that reason Tomlinson defends the ideal of 'ethical glocalism'; an preoccupation with the world and social problems which combines both perspectives: the interest in the local life world but taking into account simultaneously common global consequences and interests.

Comparing the different authors on this topic, I prefer Ulrich Beck, who since his 'cosmopolitan manifesto' not only uses cosmopolitanism as an analytical tool but also as a political program.[31] He agrees with the other sociologists that cosmopolitanism is an attitude, and certainly indispensable for social scientists. But it is more, not only a disposition, but also a changing social position. Social understanding of reality is only possible from a global perspective, not from a national view point. Why? Because our own positions and experiences of reality have changed. Our everyday life, like the music we listen to, the TV programs that we watch and the food we eat, are influenced by global processes. 'What appears as and is proclaimed as national is, in essence, increasingly transnational or cosmopolitan'.[32] (We have studied those processes in the chapters 3 and 4). Beck recognizes that social life today is still filtered through nation-state institutions what explains the contradictory nature of transnational – national relations, but what matters is the glocalisation process and its influence on social reality. Globalisation is a dialectic process in which the global and the local exist as combined and mutually implicating principles. This means that everybody's position in society is changing and of course this should imply a different attitude: a cosmopolitan perspective. Beck calls this perspective a dialogic imagination based on the coexistence of rival ways of life in the individual experience, combining contradictory certainties. The national perspective is a 'mono-logic imagination, which excludes the otherness of the other'. Concretely it means that the Dutch debate on national norms is a rear guard action, a struggle lost in advance. At the other hand exist the need for global political order. Some of this future institution are already visible: the persecution of Pinochet has been the first time that international right was more important than national right.

May be some of the readers tend to consider this cosmopolitan approach as wishful thinking. I agree that it is an ideal. But what is life without dreams? The Dutch sociologist De Swaan has studied the development of human solidarity as a process that took centuries: from consanguinity and kin as principle of communion, to neighbourhood and finally to nation, including always more people and bypassing the need for face to face contact. History shows that human solidarity has always embraced broader groups of people. De Swaan defines identification with others as an emotional process, in which people get the feeling that some are different and other are like them.[33] The first forms of identification have been based on consanguinity . With the expansion of agriculture next to consanguinity, also proximity became a criterion to identify with others. Many centuries later at the same time as the emergence of the nation state, a new and wider form of identification has emerged: nationalism. Up till now all those forms of identification go together with excluding others. If people identify as cosmopolitans, identifying with humanity in the broadest sense, exclusion is not any longer necessary. Why should this situation in which nobody is excluded, be impossible? Anyhow, the ongoing globalisation process is excluding nobody! Intercultural competence is possible only when we use more and better parameters than national cultures. Communication's cultural context can also be the neighbourhood, specific cultural fields and increasingly world-wide networks.

Notes

1. Benedict Anderson (1991) *Imagined communities*. London, Verso.

2. James Kennedy. Old and new forms of tolerance in the USA and The Netherlands in: Marcel ten Hoove (2002) *De lege tolerantie. Over vrijheid e vijblijvendheid in Nederland*. Amsterdam, Boon.

3. J. Vossenstein (2005) *Dealing with the Dutch*. Amsterdam, KIT Publishers; Janin Hunt (2002*) Culture Shock: The Netherlands*, Times Media private Limited; H. van der Horst. (2001) *The low sky*. Den Haag; W. Shetter. (1987) *The Netherlands in Perspective*. Leiden.

4. Janin o.c. p. 20.

5. G. van den Brink (2004) *Schets van een beschavingsoffensief*. Amsterdam University Press. p.107

6. Umberto Melotti (1997) International migration in Europe: social projects and political cultures in: T.Moddo and P. Werner (1997) The *politics of multiculturalism in the New Europe*. London/New York, Zed Books.

7. John Rath (1991*) Minorisering: de sociale de sociale constructie van ethnische minderheden*. Amsterdam, SUA

8. Imadele Kaka en Hatice Kursun (eds.)(2002) *Mijn geloof en mijn geluk*. Amsterdam, Schorer boeken.

9. Gert Hekma (2004) *Homoseksualiteit in Nederland van 1730 tot de moderne tijd*. Amsterdam, Meulenhoff.

10. C. van Praag Nederland als zelfbenoemde multiculturele samenleving in: R.P. Hortulanus en J.E.M. Michielse (eds.) (2002).*De multiculturele uitdaging*. Den Haag, Elsevier.

11. Arnold Reyndorp (2004) *Stadswijk* Rotterdam, Nai Uitgevers,

12. M. Verkuyten (1997) *Redelijk racisme*, gesprekken over allochtonen in oude stadswijken. Amsterdam, University press (see also Cultural discourses in the Netherlands: talking about ethnic minorities in the city. Identities 1997) 4/1: 99-132).

13. Verkuyten o.c. p.82

14. Verkuyten o.c. pp. 86-87.

15. Quoted by M. Schouten (1994) *Kleur; blank bruin & zwart in Nederland*. Amsterdam, de Bezige Bij. p.17

16. Philomena Essed. (1991) *Inzicht in het alledaags racisme*. Utrecht, Spectrum. (*Everyday Racism*)

17. Ruben Gowricharn. Openbare stekeligheid in: Hortelanius and J. Michielse. *De multiculturele uitdaging*. Pp. 55-62.

18. Gowricharn o.c. p.59

19. Portes and Lingxin Hao (2002) Fluent bi-linguism is possible among second generation and preferable than assimilation, what implies loosing competence in the own mother tongue.

20. First one to summarize and analyse the concept of transnational communities: Alejandro Portes Characteristics:

> 1. tied to the logic of capitalism (push and pull factors, scarcity of cheap labour for menial jobs and spread of consumption ideal)
>
> 2. different from former forms of immigrant adaptation
>
> 3. Broader field for popular initiatives based on innovations in communication and transportation

21. Comparative study on Iranian refugees in USA (California) and the Netherlands (Amsterdam) sample of 20 women each. Sense of belonging, feeling at home can be national or transnational; meaning home is the nation of origin, versus home can be everywhere where you feel at home. Home has a territorial meaning versus a subjective feeling; it can be everywhere.

Outcome: identification depending also on local circumstances. All women as Marxist already an international orientation. But because the social environment in California was more open to foreigners, women felt more at home than in Amsterdam, where they remained outsiders and linked to country of origin. Another study has been done by a team of the Rotterdam University.

22. A pioneer is Mohammed Arkoun (1993) *Islam in discussie* Amsterdam, Contact (Orig. Ouvertures sur l'Íslam 1989)

23. Karen Phalet (2003) De constructie van ethnische religieuze identiteit en alteriteit. In: M.C.Foblets and E.Cornelis (eds) *Migratie zijn wij uw kinderen?* Leuven/Leusden, Acco, 2003 pp. 155-184

24. Anthony Giddens (1992) *The transformation of intimacy*; sexuality love & eroticism in modern societies. Cambridge, Polity Press.

25. Judith Butler. (1997) *Excitable speech: a politics of the performative*. London, Routledge,.

26. Pierre Bourdieu. *La domination masculine*. Paris, Seuil, 1998.

27. Ash Amin (2004) Multi-ethnicity and the idea of Europe. in *Theory, Culture and Society* 21/2 April 2004 pp.1-25

28. The ideas developed in Han Entzinger and Jelle van der Meer (eds) *grenzeloze solidariteit*, to open up The Dutch society to temporary immigrants under conditions seems more realistic.

29. Ulf Hannerz cosmopolitans and locals in world culture in: M. Featherstone (ed.) Global culture nationalism, globalisation and modernity. London, Sage, 1990: 237-251. Idem. Cultural complexity New York, Columbia University Press, 1992.

30. John Tomlinson. (1999) *Globalization and culture*. Cambridge, Polity Press.

31. Ulrich Beck Cosmopolitan manifesto. In: *New Statesman* 20 March 1998 9; see also internet. Just a quote: 'The Communist Manifesto was published 150 years ago. Today, at the beginning of a new millennium, it is time for a Cosmopolitan Manifesto The Communist Manifesto was about class conflict. The Cosmopolitan Manifesto is about transnational-national conflict and dialogue which has to be opened up and organised. What is this global dialogue to be about? About the goals, values and structures of a cosmopolitan society. About whether democracy will be possible in a global age.'

32. Ulrich Beck. (2002) The cosmopolitan society and its enemies. In: *Theory, Culture and Society* 19/1-2 Febr. April 2002 pp 17-44.

33. Abraham de Swaan. (1995) Widening circles of identification: emotional concerns in sociogenic perspective. In: *Theory, Culture and Society* 12/2 pp. 25-39.

FOR FURTHER READING

Beck Ulrich (2002) 'The cosmopolitan society and its enemies'. In: *Theory, Culture and Society* 19/1-2 Febr. April 2002 pp. 17-44.

Bourdieu, Pierre (1998) *La domination masculine*. Paris, Seuil.

Bourdieu, Pierre (1986) *Distinction; a social critique of the judgement of taste*. London/New York. Routledge/Kegan Paul.

Featherstone, Mike (ed.) (1990) *Global culture nationalism, globalisation and modernity*. London, Sage.

Featherstone Mike and Scott Lash (eds.) (1999) *Spaces of culture; City-nation-World*. London/Thousand Oaks, Sage.

Giddens, Anthony (1992) *The transformation of intimacy*; sexuality love & eroticism in modern societies. Cambridge, Polity Press.

Goffman, Erving (1987) (first imp: 1959) *The presentation of self in everyday life*. London, Penguin.

Gudykunst, William B. (1998) *Bridging differences; effective intergroup communication*. Thousand Oak/London, Sage.

Hannerz, Ulf (1992) *Cultural complexity*. New York, Columbia University Press.

Kaufman, Jean-Claude (1997) *Le coeur a l'ouvrage; theorie de l'action menagere*. Paris, Nathan.

Stevenson, Nick (ed.)(2001) *Culture & Citizenship*. London, Thousand Oaks, Sage.

Tomlinson John (1999) *Globalization and culture*. Cambridge, Polity Press.

INDEX

Dealing with the Dutch

Jacob Vossestein

Whether you are coming to the Netherlands on a business trip or to work there for a while, or have regular contact with Dutch people in your own country, being prepared for Dutch culture will make your stay more effective and your interactions more satisfactory.

People from all corners of the world involved in government, business, academic studies and culture come into contact with the Dutch and may be frustrated by their directness, their critical attitude, and their sometimes slow decision-making processes – just a few of the characteristics that are immediately noticed. Fortunately, there are many good attributes, too.

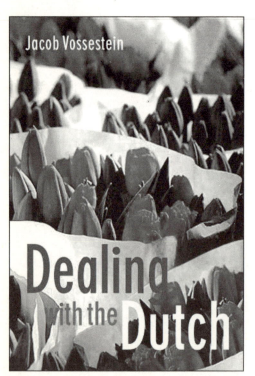

'The most concise, clearly written book on the subject available.'
Amazon

'Vossestein uses quotes from foreigners, which is entertaining and effective.'
NRC Handelsblad

'Vossestein takes a light-hearted look at the way the Dutch live and work.'
Made in Holland

ISBN 90 6832 565 5 • 14th updated edition • KIT Publishers • paperback